T0370424

TIME

THE GREAT EQUALIZER

DR. JOHN D. MCCONNELL

authorHOUSE®

AuthorHouse™
1663 Liberty Drive
Bloomington, IN 47403
www.authorhouse.com
Phone: 833-262-8899

Published by AuthorHouse 06/18/2024

ISBN: 979-8-8230-2830-1 (sc)
ISBN: 979-8-8230-2829-5 (e)

Library of Congress Control Number: 2024911618

Print information available on the last page.

CONTENTS

CONTENTS

DEDICATION

I dedicate this book to my sons, Jarrett and Jadden McConnell. Because of you, my life has reason. No award or accolade can compete with my joy that comes from being your dad. While developing this book about TIME, I realized the value of every moment we've had together. I don't believe in wasted moments. All time is significant when we are intentional. One of the biggest reasons I strive to never stop producing, is so you guys won't be disappointed in me. I'm not ashamed to admit that I spent many years parenting afraid. I didn't always know if there'd be enough – or if I was enough. Although sometimes it's a struggle, I'm learning to celebrate your decisions, instead of hovering. I'm proud of the men you've become, and I hope (through this book) you realize that you must remain available for all of the different levels of growth awaiting you. I am living out loud in front of you on purpose so that you can see that living a good life isn't measured only by the number of good days you have. The moment you turn your tests into testimonies, they no longer have power over you. We grow accustomed to the traditional parent role of being there for our kids, sometimes unaware they are here for us. I see you walking in your purpose men of God - shoulders above the negative stereotypes that have imprisoned so many young men. I'm great with who you are! Thanks for being there for me through all of life's transitions.

NOTE FROM AUTHOR

Plato, an ancient Greek philosopher, said "Necessity is the mother of invention". Everything and everyone has a purpose and reason for existing. No matter how insignificant, roles matter. On average, the lifespan of a worker honeybee is less than two months. Between nursing the colony, cleaning the hive, and foraging nectar to make honey, every honeybee has a job to do. The goal of pollination is the successful transfer of pollen between flowers of the same plant species leading to fertilization, seed development, and fruit production. If bees, birds, bats, butterflies, and beetles don't enforce pollination, fertilization cannot take place. Even the wind is an important component.

Choosing not to embrace your purpose, does not excuse you from it. We're all here for a reason, and those reasons are seeking out each and every one of us. Stepping up to be the parent, entrepreneur, or leader you intend to be, is a choice you must make that will impact the balance of your days.

Our relationship with time is just as complicated as our relationships with individuals. Many of the same things ring true. With both, it's impossible to wipe the slate clean and start over. Time and people are impacted by the choices we make. Both constantly change, and are never found standing still. Time is something we cannot alter, but with more understanding of it, we can begin to fare better. It's clever to imagine someone finding their place in time. It almost sounds like a play on words. We obviously play no role in becoming alive, but piecing the edges together for how you best fit is attainable. As I began noticing moments of reflection and regret, conversations started in my head. Those conversations have become the pages of this book. I don't offer this manuscript as a solution or code for understanding time, but as a conversation starter. How we regard time determines how we use it. Let's put it under a microscope and learn a little more about it.

CHAPTER 1

BECOMING AVAILABLE

Although we fight to be seen a certain way, life has its own method of presenting us. How we wish to be seen and the way we're actually viewed can be polar differences from each other. In our early years, we latch on and identify with the first thing that excites us. With the help of cosigners, we begin labeling ourselves. We apply undue pressure to make our self-imposed labels successful. What you don't realize at the age of nineteen is that new layers will be added each year. As we're maturing, we are still becoming. We are not simply one thing with one layer. We are to be a multifaceted masterpiece. As long as I remain engaged, who I am at twenty-six will be different than who I am at thirty-six, forty-six, sixty-six, or seventy-six. Because of how life is set up, we feel forced to identify ourselves with labels. The more we evolve, the more difficult it should be to answer the question of who we are. Today

Dr. John D. McConnell

as a fifty-six-year-old man, I am an author, singer, songwriter, playwright, Christian counselor worship-leader, and father. My list was shorter thirty years ago. To be clear, this isn't solely about age. With age should come deeper understanding, but depending on your journey, the number of roles you have aren't restricted by age.

Having vs Fulfilling

Something important we have no clue about in our youth is the distinction between having roles and fulfilling them. Every teacher I ever had was an actual teacher of record, but only about half of them fulfilled the role in my opinion. The world is filled with women and men who have children. But we factually know the role of parent has grossly been unfulfilled in many homes. Some qualifications don't become authentic simply from logged hours and observations.

Some roles require a heart connection to accompany the certification.

Don't be thrown off or angered when the label you're marketing isn't sticking. How we're trying rigorously to be known, may not be how we'll want to be known later. Sometimes it can feel more like a curse to be known all over the world. When people become famous for something, it's difficult for them to become anything else. A concern many actors have is being typecasted. The majority of Julia Roberts' roles depict her as a no-nonsense woman with a heart of gold - a beautiful woman with a hard exterior. Although she is an extremely successful movie star, it may be difficult for her to be successfully cast as a different type of character going forward. We've seen examples of child stars who turn to negative behaviors, such as addictions - due to the pressures of trying to sustain a lifestyle that represents a fictitious character people grew up watching on television. Everyone should be entitled to experience the changing seasons of their life away from the scrutiny of others.

Who we really are is still taking form. However, we must avail ourselves to the process. A work of art, though beautiful in the end, is the painstaking result of war.

I'll never be the sum of all my experiences, but the product of how they affected me. Shampoo products are created to clean hair follicles, while depositing nutrients to support and sustain new hair growth. When we audition hair products, we look intently to notice their effects. One may cause irritation to my scalp, while another may prompt my hair to thin. In an ideal world, this process ends with finding a shampoo that satisfies our needs. Similarly over the course of years, many circumstances and situations are introduced and sometimes infused into our lives. Unlike shampoo, it's impossible to completely wash away the imprints of our connections. One can never be untouched once touched.

There is a phrase basketball players yell when they think the referee gets the call wrong. If a player disputes having fouled an opponent, and the free-throw shots are missed, you can always hear someone shout, "ball don't lie". The narrative is that even if the referee makes a mistake, the basketball will judge the decision fairly. One doesn't have to believe in a basketball god to follow that logic.

Blood also does not lie. A short time ago I got news that someone I grew up with passed away unexpectedly. Apparently, he was driving to an appointment, started feeling bad, and had the presence of mind to pull his vehicle over to the side of the road. He lost consciousness, and a passerby phoned in a medical emergency. Over the next two weeks, he never regained consciousness and died. The doctors determined that he had AVM. Although he never experienced prior symptoms, he lived with this vascular anomaly in his bloodstream for sixty-three years.

An arterial venous malformation is an abnormal connection between arteries and veins, bypassing the capillary system. Most often the person is born with AVMs but they can appear shortly after birth or later in life.

Perhaps the doors that won't open for us are not intended for us to walk through. Sometimes I feel an overwhelming responsibility to make it all makes sense. At times we try to control things that are out of our hands. The absolute best we can do in any situation is to stand up and not shrink. Does it mean we're getting it wrong when the access to things we desire is repeatedly denied? When we can't identify the culprit, that's the story so many of us tell ourselves. But why can't we accept that no one and no thing is at fault? Must there always be a fall guy when things don't turn out exactly according to our plan? We live in seasons, where relationships, investments, and outcomes go bad, despite all the right moves. These are the toughest instances to console, as we're always looking for an appropriate response. We must condition ourselves to become recipients of grace - not so much from others as from ourselves. The period of mourning things that haven't worked out shouldn't last too long. We risk becoming a victim by feeling sorry for ourselves. Professional boxers master the art of bobbing and weaving. They don't fight with the expectation of never being hit. Their training focuses on reducing a direct punch

 Dr. John D. McConnell

to the category of a lesser glancing blow. Unless we learn to become more accepting of the scripts for our lives to constantly change, we can never anticipate the power of the next punch. Victory is determined by who's still standing at the end of each round.

As I pay attention to my life, I begin to realize more and more that much of the anxiety I feel is self-induced. I've been making life a fight, and it's not that at all. We enter this fascinating world, and begin endless discovery. Our exploration incites an awakening of ourselves. Once we become alive to our desires, the battle begins. Although we were created to have free will, the intention of our creator has always been for us to want what's already been chosen for us. Why that sounds complicated is the very reason our fight with life ensues. At the end of our road, there is a sense of pride in recalling sacrifices we made to cause things to turn out as well as they did. I contend that we end life exactly as ultimately intended. Yes, we had to make the choices to engage the law of cause and effect, but the outcome was always going to be the same. Aristotle asserted that we live in a world governed by law, and that everything happens for a reason whether or not we know what it is. It's been speculated that the average person will make nearly eight hundred thousand decisions over a lifetime and will come to regret about one hundred forty-four thousand of them. I believe the pressure of believing we're responsible for our lives puts us on the path to becoming. Whether we support or regret our decisions, ours feels like a lifelong battle - especially when we fight against who we'll ultimately be once it's all figured out.

Continue flinging your aspirations against the wall to see what sticks. Stop apologizing for changing your mind. If today reveals

Dr. John D. McConnell

something you never knew before, doesn't that qualify you to rework your position? We are more complicated than we give ourselves credit for. And the more we learn about ourselves, the more accountable we should be. People usually get what they expect. There's a heightened awareness for it. Being offended, not being paid what you're worth, and being passed over for a promotion, are only a few examples of expectations people walk around with. Why are we expecting things not to change, when they always do? Fulfillment today does not mean fulfillment tomorrow for that simple reason. Because I've already experienced the fascination of today, tomorrow must impress me with a new surprise.

We must get acquainted with a new story. In this version, we don't look back to who we used to be with nostalgia. We eagerly embrace what's ahead of us because we realize it will soon be a steppingstone as well. Accommodating what's next supports our stance for remaining available. If we have no vacancy for what may be coming towards us, we will most certainly forfeit its potential impact on our lives. The things we fail to be available for, are most likely the injections our lives need.

Never Say Never

Today is the day I never saw coming. Have you ever disqualified yourself prematurely? We can get it in our head that we're not what they're looking for. No matter how many qualifiers we have, some of us are excellent at removing ourselves from contention. Something caused us to regard what we have, or who we are as being inferior. Some things we view as a competition only require our participation. How can you know where you stand if you don't show up?

Dr. John D. McConnell

When I first began this chapter, I was only considering the many ways I needed to work on making myself available to the constant flow of life. But every coin has two sides. We must embrace our attributes that are good, while being watchful for situations to bend towards us. Years ago, there were women who I considered to be "out of my league". Actually, it wasn't only my consideration – they told me as much. My attempt is not to generalize or stereotype any group of women, so let me be clear that I am actually talking about the same women. Be true to who you are because over time things change. We have this idea in our mind of the type of person we'd like to spend our life with. We are so bold as to make a list. There's nothing wrong with seeking a type. Everybody does it - yes, guys too. After we marry the illusion of what we thought we wanted, the reality of what we need becomes exposed. Some women who would never give me the time of day, now entertain my friendship. The point I'm making is, never stop leading with those things you know are great about you. Don't try to make yourself fit who you want. They already want you – even if they don't know it yet.

Have you ever walked into a room in the middle of a conversation you thought was about you - only to find out later that it wasn't? Sometimes we misjudge moments and respond in ways we wish we could take back. How about the moments when we fail to say anything at all? An opportunity to speak on someone's behalf may afford us only a very small window. However, the repercussion for our silence could haunt us for eternity. When I was a classroom teacher, it was once alleged by a coworker that I had used inappropriate force when disciplining a student in my classroom. I was placed on suspension and denied access to my campus, pending an investigation. When the student was questioned regarding my conduct, he told the truth. My career and integrity as a Texas certified teacher relied on his truth being heard. It was the difference between my suspension being lifted, and my being terminated. Who's relying on you to advocate on their behalf? What have you witnessed that only your words will bring resolution to?

All the crime drama shows we see on television aren't fictitious. Many are based on real life occurrences. According to the National Registry of Exonerations, nearly six hundred wrongly convicted people have been exonerated based on DNA tests that demonstrated their innocence. How devastated would you be if a rape victim picked you out of a lineup, saying you raped her? An eyewitness statement is damning, depending on who you are in the scenario.

Disregarding a victim's first-hand account of their own experience is not a practice. In fact, a prosecutor's terminology for having an eyewitness, is called a "slam dunk". Amazingly, trauma can distort memory. Some empowerment for moving beyond traumatic events comes from closure. What if when we think we're setting things right, we're actually setting things wrong? Imagine being snatched from your family and locked in a prison for twenty years for something you had nothing to do with. Now imagine being the one pointing the finger of accusation. No one goes free in this episode, except the person never brought to trial. In a scenario like this, I'd like to think the rapist has never experienced absolution. Time has many labels, one of which I call "Reaper". We must account for the things we do, and we never go free without asking for forgiveness. When we cause harm, we experience a torturous

 Dr. John D. McConnell

unrest unless or until we make things right. Evaluate your unrest and use the time you have to restore peace to your life. Although New York's Metropolitan Transportation Authority's slogan wasn't crafted for this purpose, I believe it's applicable – "See something – say something".

What's the forecast?

Most every evening, I ask Google for tomorrow's weather forecast. Having at least a general idea of how cold it will be guides me in selecting the outfit I'll pull from my closet. As we know, the forecast isn't always completely accurate. A thunderstorm can be heading in my direction, but by morning the winds can push it several hundred miles away. The science of any forecast is based on projections and probabilities. The April 8, 2024, media coverage of the total eclipse was astounding. Mathematical calculations empowered ABC to capture real-time images of the total solar eclipse in fifteen cities along its path from Mazatlán, Mexico to Quebec, Canada. If we're capable of predicting occurrences two hundred thirty-nine thousand miles outside of our own orbit, why are we so oblivious to the destruction our negative lifestyles perpetuate? Because of our intelligence, time for mankind should be considered a gift. When our analytics show us the dangers ahead, why do we stay the course? Animals only have intuition, but humans have intuition, data, science, history, and innovation. Just like with DNA and the Innocence Project, each year our technological advances reduce our margins for error in so many disciplines. Life insurance companies are already using behavioral research data to increase their accuracy in predicting how long we'll live. The secrets are out, so pay attention to what's being forecasted.

Dr. John D. McConnell

Stop telling people who you are, and begin showing them. What you represent should be more important than what you call yourself.

How valuable is a name?

In the early 1920s, sixty or more Osage people in Osage County, Oklahoma were reported murdered within a short period of time. It was reported as the "reign of terror" on the Osage Reservation. The deaths were associated with several members of one family. The tribe had retained mineral rights to the valuable land of their reservation. The deaths were suspiciously misreported and covered up by individuals who were heirs (by marriage) to the future fortunes.

When Africans were taken into slavery beginning in 1619, they were stripped of their names. Even in prisons today, inmates are recognized by a number, rather than the name given to them by their parents. It's because of these types of situations, many people are so invested in the pride of their name. It's innate to be protective of anything that's being stolen from you. Slaves of back then and inmates of now learned a lesson the whole world can stand to learn as well. No institution, government, system, or individual can make us forget who we are. How we live exemplifies who we live for. Our actions say more about who we are than our name ever will. Many of us have not been the franchise player, CEO, or CFO, but we're just as essential to the team. I can only imagine how awesome it would feel to hear a stadium of fans shouting my name. Nevertheless, I can always walk with my head held high if I know I'm living with integrity. Whether or not our name is on the back of our jersey for everyone to see, our reward should be to help our fellow man.

 Dr. John D. McConnell

CHAPTER 2

START SOMETHING
WORTH FINISHING

There is a quote that says, "Find a job you love, and you will never have to work a day in your life." Purpose in life doesn't come from obligations we have, but from desires that grow along the way. When people are forced to make decisions they're not ready for, things are added to their life they may be unable to support. We are guilty a lot of times of making ill-advised stops along the route to our destiny. It's tough navigating when you're not completely sure where you're headed. We don't always know the type of people we should or should not connect to until our interactions with them become part of our experience. Even the most perceptive people can't solely rely on their ability to analyze a situation from a distance. Living life fully involves risk - and some of the risks we take are joined to us forever. There may be several effects our behaviors have caused

Dr. John D. McConnell

to be added to us, such as alimony, child-support, mortgages, or bankruptcy.

We rarely forsake the commitments we value. Successfully raising a child from infancy to adulthood, or being able to burn the mortgage on a home, are just a few examples of vows people pledge their lives to accomplish. Countless times have I heard stories about elderly couples who die within weeks of each other. It's almost like they've made a pact to be there for one another until the end. After one let's go, the other feels as though they've fulfilled their assignment. Is it the length of our assignments that determine how long we'll remain in the earth?

The Bible says God tasked Noah to build an ark in preparation of a great flood. The instructions included dimensions just shy of the length of two NFL football fields. Historians postulate that it took Noah and his family seventy-five to one hundred twenty years to build the ark. How many years do you need to get your work done?

When we submit to a vision or goal, it's easy to get lost within it. The jobs we take are not the same as the jobs that take us. Those things we don't have passion for become heavy weights around our neck. We become clock-watchers, and are never unsuspecting when it's time for our work shift to end. A vocation our heart is drawn to ceases to be just a job. Even when the shift ends, it's work we take home with us. The intrinsic motivation keeps the fire burning night and day. When there's purpose for each day, it inspires movement and activity. Health professionals say if you live a sedentary lifestyle, you have a higher chance of experiencing depression and anxiety, being overweight, and developing type two diabetes or heart disease. Happiness derives from the quality of life we're leading. Focusing on living more, empowers us to live longer.

 Dr. John D. McConnell

What prevents us from following through on what we've started? Our society has become crippled by its own greed and feelings of entitlement. There have never been more programs, from social justice to affordable Wi-Fi connectivity. Whereas I celebrate our nation's growth in acknowledging inclusion and many other civil and socioeconomic disparities, it has created some loopholes. We are now living in a culture of dependency. Labels that were created out of a need to secure grants and funding have become badges some are proud to wear. What used to be regarded as God's hand at work to extend favor, has become an expectation of what is owed. Everyone should be so fortunate to have grandparents who tell stories of their childhood with added hyperbole. They tell their story of having had to walk uphill ten miles to and from school in a foot of snow, to shut down your whiny complaint of your mom being late picking you up from a friend's house. Where is the grit once known as pride, for making one's own way? Necessary government funding is now on the chopping blocks because millions of people have learned how to manipulate the system. Of course, this doesn't apply to everyone, but if it's you, own it. It's easier sometimes to get a doctor to diagnose your child with ADHD, than to enforce strict behavioral strategies. As someone who invested twenty-seven years as a classroom teacher, I offered hundreds of hours of input regarding Individualized Education Programs (IEPs). Although necessary for the majority of kids who have one, this legal document enforces modifications that affirm entitlement some children may never disassociate from. Modifications include being given an extended amount of time to complete classroom assignments and

Dr. John D. McConnell

tests. Students may be offered hard copies of teacher notes – in addition to handouts provided to all students. Children with IEPs may also be given breaks other students don't receive, and afforded opportunities to work in less populated areas of the campus. As a community, we all have a role in producing adults who make us proud of our society. Malnourishment is a direct reflection of diet. Sustainability and sustenance go hand-in-hand.

Are we not finishing because we've not been taught how? It must be addressed. Have we lived so long receiving modifications, that we don't know how to apply ourselves to finish tasks? It's very difficult to provide a system of discipline if you're not a product of it. There are many things we start that are definitely worth finishing. But you must discover what makes you fall short.

Who and what you're connected to

determine where you're going. I am fascinated by unlikely partnerships that yield great triumphs. NBA great Robert Horry most likely wouldn't be as well known today, had he not been an outstanding system player. System players have a few key roles, that if they do well, make them irreplaceable. Robert Horry was nicknamed "Big-shot Bob" because he had a talent for shooting and scoring the deep ball in crucial moments to win high-stake games. Amazingly, he has seven championship rings from three different NBA teams - with no defeats in NBA finals. Finding the right fit is crucial to identifying the purpose for your life.

NFL Hall of Fame wide receiver, Chris Carter, was asked to speak at the 2010 NFL Rookie Symposium. In his speech, he cautioned players to separate themselves from unsavory distractions off the field. He shared his personal story of negative behavior that threatened to end his career. The New England Patriot's fourth round draft pick, Aaron Hernandez, asked the first question. "What changes did you make from when you got cut by the Eagles to when you went to Minnesota?" Carter replied, "You gotta get your stuff together and stop lying to yourself. I stopped smoking that dope and started getting my body in shape to be able to run all day. I told my old friends, don't call me. This should be the fork in the road for a lot of y'all to get your stuff together before you get popped - because you're gonna get caught. You're gonna get caught"! After only three seasons and a brand new forty-million-dollar contract, Aaron Hernandez got caught living way beneath his privilege. Hernandez was arrested for murder, found guilty, and given a life sentence. Less than four years later, he committed suicide in prison.

We can't always be the headliner. After

all, it's the supporting cast that causes the headliner to shine. If you've ever witnessed a one-man show, undoubtedly your attention was drawn to the deficits. The jobs of selling tickets, running lights, wardrobe, and sound must be covered. Becoming a very functional part of a thriving system is important. We must know what goes into making a production its very best. Those details are only revealed behind-the-scenes. There's no way to know just how far your function will carry your organization, so begin by plugging in. Every time pride lifts its head, evaluate what your role means to the team, and what the team means to you.

Your perception will always determine how you prioritize. Whatever we consider important usually gets our attention. At times our lives become so busy that we mishandle some of the things we're juggling. Our children feel unsupported when we

Dr. John D. McConnell

stop showing up at their games. Our spouse feels neglected when we stop checking in as often as we used to. It's not intentional, but a common issue most adults must confront as our responsibilities increase. We are great at starting strong, but finishing is not something many of us are very familiar with. It's like the episode from the Cosby show when Heathcliff reminded Theo of all the instruments in the basement he and his siblings once purposed to learn to play, but eventually chucked them to the side. We move on sometimes, even in the process of a thing. You know what they say… "Divorce happens long before the divorce". We don't even prioritize our health the way we should. I tell the story often. that not even the diagnosis of diabetic retinopathy caused me to change my lifestyle. It took losing thirty percent of my vision to force me on the road to lose one hundred fifteen pounds. Yes – that

I finished! Perhaps experiencing a great loss is what you need to help you prioritize your commitments. Things worth finishing are things that would create voids if they were not there. Start initiatives that become so important, you can't live without them. You mustn't allow boredom to take root. It's a trick to make you devalue what you already know is important.

The recent upheaval regarding abortion rights in large part is due to the unfathomable number of women who choose to abort their babies. The ticker has increased to just shy of one million abortions performed each year in the US. The astounding number completely removes the focus from birth defects, rape, and incest to a blatant disregard for life. A woman's right to govern her body should be her decision alone, but how did we get here? The largest percentage of that big number is created by people who don't count the cost before engaging in sexual intercourse. I won't use this platform to promote one argument over the other. However, it is my opinion that it is morally wrong to do nothing to rectify what has become a pattern of genocide.

Choosing To Parent

The decision to bring life into the world is a lifetime commitment. We don't get to choose when our children will no longer need us to be the voice in their ear. We are always to be responsible for our children. If we don't effectively teach them to contribute positively to society, their shortcomings are our shortcomings.

James and Jennifer Crumbley, parents of a fifteen-year-old school shooter in Michigan, were charged with manslaughter and sentenced to serve ten to fifteen years in prison. If we equip our children to cause harm, are we not partners in the misery they cause?

If we empower them to be a blessing, don't we also deserve to be part of the celebration? Parenting is something that requires us to finish. Anything less is unreasonable and a disservice to our code as human beings. Parenting is a tremendous sacrifice. It asks of you at the most inopportune moments. You can never be too tired to fulfill your role. If you've not yet decided that parenting is worth finishing, don't start.

There is a show I've enjoyed watching for several years starring Tom Selleck, called Blue Bloods. It's about a New York police family. Four generations of New York police officers are chronicled in this drama. The Reagans, an Irish family, flaunt the traditions that make them as close knit as they are. I am particularly drawn to the manner in which most episodes have concluded over the show's fourteen seasons. Without fail, every Sunday afternoon, the Reagans gather at the family house for dinner. It's not just about the food, but they use the gathering as a "check in". They laugh, squabble, bicker, and fight. But the most important thing is that they come together to love on one another.

Psalms 133:1 says,
"How good and pleasant it is when God's people live together in unity!"

What traditions do you have that keep you connected to the communities you value? The pace of the world moves so quickly, and if we don't have routines for fellowship, some of our necessary lifelines can be choked out. Institute road trips, cruises, and annual reunions to safeguard the bonds you have with those you love.

I'll use a very literal example to conclude this chapter. If you've ever built something with your own hands, you know the pride you feel from beginning to end. In its infancy, a backyard shed doesn't resemble a shed at all. It looks like a perfectly poured concrete slab, intentionally placed near the fence line. That's what your neighbor sees. But you, your wife, and kids see so much more. Those in your house see more because your excitement has been leaking out of you. It's difficult to keep something you're excited about a secret. Already you see the ten-foot roof with designer shingles. You can see the tall barn doors that swing outward. You imagine the white shelves along the back wall, above the lawnmower and snowblower. It will be a few months before it's finished, but you saw it complete long before you ever broke ground. Details matter the most. If they don't jump out at you before you get started, it's hard to know where the motivation will come from to finish. Growing up, my dad had cleaning contracts with about five office buildings in

Kansas City. My siblings and I joined the workforce around the age of twelve. My dad had this saying, "Get them with the floors". He taught us how to use industrial buffers to clean, strip, and polish floors. Over time, high traffic floors without carpet become dingy and dull in appearance. With the right cleaning products and a buffer, you can restore flooring to its original look. A mistake amateurs make is to stop there. Without a protective FINISH, everything you've done to restore beauty and luster will be lost in a matter of days. Your work must be sealed and finished with a protective wax.

The finishing details are rarely free flowing when the idea or project isn't really worth going all the way. Time misused isn't very forgiving. Stop doing things strictly from a perspective of obligation, and dive into things that bring you joy. You're not always going to be able to justify why it's important to you. Some stories make more sense when told backwards. Your reason for doing something might not show you its logic until after you've completed it. All you may know about it now is that it's worth seeing it to its completion.

Dr. John D. McConnell

CHAPTER 3

LIVING BEYOND
BAD DECISIONS

What qualifies someone to be called a good decision-maker? How often do we have to get it wrong before losing the trust of those depending on us? I lost count years ago of the number of stupid choices I've made. One of the difficult things about being a decision-maker is not knowing if you've made the right one until later. It seems unfair to be judged by outcomes we must predict. No one escapes the role of becoming a chooser, but some do it far better than others. The gravity of our decisions often determine our comfort level. In my twenties, at the beginning of my marriage, my wife was in charge of managing our budget. It wasn't because of any particular reason, other than to mimic the roles I saw my mom and dad play. Once I discovered that she was uncomfortable with the task, and using the 'Eenie Meanie Miny Moe' approach to paying our bills, we shifted our roles according to stress level.

Dr. John D. McConnell

Don't allow your past decisions to judge your future. We formulate our choices with the information available to us. Part of that resource bank is our experience. The more we live, the more knowledgeable we become. No matter how bad a mistake we've made, it's imperative we learn to trust ourselves. No man should be an island to himself. Having confidence for making good decisions is strengthened by paying attention to the decisions others make. Watch your mentors closely and take advantage of being able to ask them questions. All decisions aren't arrived at easily, and just because you make the right ones, isn't a guarantee of happiness.

Cultivating self-compassion is key. Beating oneself up over past mistakes only perpetuates negative feelings and can hinder progress. Instead, practice self-forgiveness and focus on moving forward with a constructive mindset. Remembering that everyone is fallible and that imperfection is a natural part of the human experience can alleviate unnecessary guilt and shame.

Embracing a growth mindset is instrumental. Viewing setbacks as opportunities for growth fosters resilience and encourages continuous improvement. Rather than seeing bad decisions as permanent failures, approach them as temporary setbacks that can be overcome with perseverance and determination. This mindset shift empowers individuals to learn from their mistakes and adapt their decision-making processes accordingly. Welcoming support from trusted friends, family members, or mentors can provide valuable perspective and guidance. Surrounding oneself with a supportive network can offer encouragement during challenging times and help navigate through tough decisions.

Admitting the need for help with making

 Dr. John D. McConnell

decisions is a crucial step towards personal growth and development. It requires humility, self-awareness, and a willingness to acknowledge one's limitations. In a world that often glorifies independence and self-sufficiency, admitting vulnerability can be challenging. The decision-making process is complex and influenced by various factors, including emotions, biases, and external pressures. Despite our best efforts, we are not always equipped to make optimal decisions on our own. This is where seeking help becomes invaluable. One of the reasons admitting the need for help with decision-making can be difficult is the fear of judgment or appearing weak. Society often associates asking for help with incompetence or inadequacy. However, this mindset is outdated and detrimental. Recognizing our limitations and seeking support demonstrates strength and wisdom. It shows that we prioritize making informed choices over preserving our ego. No one has all the answers, and by acknowledging this, we create space for collective problem-solving and innovation. Seeking help with decision-making is an act of self-care. It acknowledges that our mental and emotional well-being are important and worth investing in. Making decisions can be stressful, especially when faced with high-stakes or uncertain situations. Having a support system in place can alleviate some of this burden and provide reassurance during challenging times.

Availing oneself of professional help from a therapist or counselor can be beneficial for processing emotions and developing healthier coping mechanisms.

Practice mindfulness and present-moment awareness. Cultivating mindfulness allows individuals to become more attuned to their thoughts, feelings, and impulses, enabling them to make more conscious and intentional decisions. By staying grounded in the present moment, individuals can better regulate their emotions and respond to situations with clarity and composure. Incorporating regular reflection and self-assessment into one's routine can help reinforce positive decision-making habits and prevent future missteps.

Some of the hardest decisions are followed by heartache and pain. It's agonizing to hurt people, but sometimes our decisions are responsible for a lot of distress. As I look back at decisions I made in the past, I can't say every decision was met with honesty. There were times I wasn't completely honest with myself, or others who may have been involved. When I knew the truth was hurtful, I looked for ways not to have to express it. If you've recognized a negative pattern in the way you make decisions, search out strategies to modify your process. Here are a few strategies I employ when making decisions.

Follow Peace

If the decision you're making causes you to be anxious and produces unrest, you've probably not arrived at the correct resolve. Once you've carefully weighed all of your options, the decision you make, should not impede your ability to relax, or carry on with other affairs.

Confide In Someone You Trust

Every now and then it's good to run your thoughts by someone in whose judgment you trust. Impartial opinions are good for noticing angles we may be too close to see.

Some therapists believe you must confess out loud what you've done as a first step towards recovery. Whether or not we can talk about it, we know what we've done. What is recovery actually?

By definition, recovery is a return to a normal state of health, mind, or strength.

Should recovery be our goal following a life landslide? A return to normalcy doesn't support an individual's quest to identify their purpose. I contend that being normal or living the status quo is the root that triggered our bad behavior. There are only three reasons for recanting our deeds out loud (compassion, comparison, or transparency).

Compassion

Some people put their dark deeds on display to illicit a response. It's sometimes a cry for help, or it can be them posturing as a victim for your sympathy.

Comparison

I'll tell mine if you tell yours. When we genuinely want to gauge our behavior, we feel better when we can judge someone else as being worse than we are.

Transparency

People often unmask to avoid awkward conversations down the road. Trusting you with my truth allows you an opportunity to decide to connect with me or walk away.

Out loud or not, permission to thrive on the other side of poor decisions, can only come from yourself. You owe no apologies to anyone. The biggest mistake one can make following bad choices, is to not learn from them. Sometimes going down the wrong road is the best lesson possible.

Are you more forgiving of yourself than of others? We may want to check that we're not holding people to hire standards than ourselves. That was an eye-opening realization I recently learned about myself. Many of us don't know how we'll react to someone disappointing us until it happens. It's difficult to set expectations for yourself, without doing the same for those connected to you. In essence, we set ourselves up for disappointment, because people can never live up to the pedestal you put them on. If we fail at accomplishing our own goals, surely we'll be let down by those with the audacity to dream their own dreams. We make the assumption that everyone in our house is completely submitted to our way of doing things. Despite our example and leadership, our children, spouse, friends, and associates will choose the life they've decided to lead. Prior to the twenty-first century, influences outside of the home were extremely limited. How to live, and what to aspire to were things you were taught, and not experientially discovered. Even without a spouse, there's no such thing as a single parent anymore. We're paying Roku and Wi-Fi to help raise our children. And those who keep their kids off the Internet make them victims of the kids who have unlimited access. Stop defining yourself by the choices others make.

Just because my children make choices outside of mine, doesn't mean it's something they need forgiveness for. What qualifies their actions as mistakes? Many of us are excluded from our children's decision-making process. It's not always that they feel you can't guide them, but your stern judgment keeps them at bay. They feel forced to make critical decisions without you because of their fear of you. We all have a need to be loved before, during, and after our decisions. Instead, we are made to feel that our decisions are wrong, and at best, only tolerated. If your

Dr. John D. McConnell

choices are never celebrated, eventually you stop making them out loud.

Investigate why you fraternize with negativity. If you consistently find yourself in compromising situations, that will always be the case - unless you do something different. We have the ability to alter our attractions. If how you choose to spend your time is harming you, you must begin choosing differently. Until we can rely on ourselves to make proficient decisions, we can't really expect anyone else to highly regard our choices. Depending on the struggle, flirting with our demons, stall our momentum towards freedom. Confront your addictions by properly addressing them. Whether it's lying, stealing, cheating, gambling, pornography, overspending, or gluttony, call it by its proper name. If we're unwilling to see things for what they truly are, we won't deal with them head-on. Not every negative behavior is an addiction, but what we fail to label, will eventually label us. Knowing your triggers makes you a very powerful person. Even if you've not yet learned to control the trigger, you know the warning signs to enforce the proper distance. As we gain more confidence for withstanding what used to topple us, we begin accepting more challenges. Time becomes our friend in this regard because only time and practice makes us better.

The euphoria one feels when they become inebriated become the breadcrumbs of an addict. To acquire a feeling unmatched by any other is rare. Recapturing it isn't only difficult, it's impossible. We must be careful not to make people idols for our illusions. They remind us of a different time and place. Our hyper creative mind has the ability to cut and paste new people into old memories. The pressure we place on idols is a standard

 Dr. John D. McConnell

they could never live up to. Unless we're striving for new experiences, we're simply swapping cast members for the same old production. It's a formula for disaster. The last cast member bailed under your pressure, and so will this one. There must be lessons learned. Instead of writing people in, turn your expectation off for a period of TIME. Welcome people into your life without forcing them to jump through hoops. You don't know what "new" feels like until you've tried it on.

Who's running the clock down on you? It's one thing to put pressure on ourselves, but it's something altogether different when someone else has a timer on us. No one gets to use the clock against us regarding our own personal growth. Life is too complicated to allow anyone to lord over us with that kind of power. We may not be where we hoped we'd be by this time in our lives, but that's the struggle everyone has on their personal journey. Why something didn't happen isn't always the result of something you did wrong. Even when you go after something in the most aggressive way, there's no guarantee you can pull it into your life. If you're anything like me, you want things to connect and have reason. Many times bitterness compounds our frustration when years later, we still can't wrap our mind around why it didn't happen. I am convinced that there are things we believe we're built for, that would devastate our lives if allowed in. What we try desperately to open the door to receive, our creator (God) denies it access to us. Sometimes we benefit from prayers that others prayed on our behalf. We can't always connect the dots to address what went wrong, but when you know you've done your part, you must trust that things will work out as they should. Be

Dr. John D. McConnell

careful of the opinions you allow to govern your steps. Only those who know you well should play a role in helping you chart your course.

CHAPTER 4

TRANSPARANCY

A byproduct of being and feeling safe is transparency. It is a gift we give ourselves and others. When collaborating, the most valuable resource available is information. Transparency is the oil that lubricates any type of relationship. There are always justifiable reasons to not disclose personal information. But as we build new alliances, the strength of their foundation will be determined by the number of walls we allow to remain standing. Many subscribe to the "don't ask – don't tell" code of conduct. What happens when pieces of your truth begin to show up? How will it affect your supposedly committed relationship? Unless you were raised in a remote community completely off the grid, you know how it feels to be lied to. When you harbor information that later becomes disclosed, little by little, you put your partner's trust in you on probation. They become watchful for other things you may not have shared, and begin constructing their own walls for protection. Maintaining trust is so much easier than the road to rebuilding it.

Not that everyone should be like me, but I believe in putting it all out there. When I feel a strong connection to someone, and believe it's potential to be lasting, I share intimate details about myself. People have lived through trauma, and I don't think it's fair to wade six months into a relationship without divulging what could potentially be red flags. Why intentionally waste someone else's time? Information is power, and it gives the other person the opportunity to dismiss it as a non-issue if that's how they perceive it. Forcing people to wait and discover our truth is painful for everyone involved. Besides, that's already going to happen regarding the flaws we've not yet learned of.

Sometimes   transparency   is

58 *Dr. John D. McConnell*

mischaracterized as a weakness. Transparency and vulnerability go hand-in-hand. It's unusual to find one without the other. Being transparent with someone is very similar to undressing in front of them. The insecurities you have about what's usually hidden, are now being placed on display. Trepidation and hesitancy consume the room you're in, no matter its size. Although what you're about to share is truth, the response to its reveal is unknown. Your choice to bear your soul will put your relationship on a totally different trajectory. It's a risk because you can't predict what will follow.

Our willingness to engage in transparency fosters open communication but also helps to nurture empathy within a relationship. Whether in our family or work settings, we are often in chronic environments of invalidation. Because of it, we grow accustomed to shutting down. Repeatedly justifying how and who we are to people who demonize us, is a movie we've already seen far too many times. As we begin feeling the reward side of unambiguity, it becomes easier to be more forthright with those in our inner circle. If we always avoid the potential downside of vulnerability, we will never experience the exhilaration that occurs when it all goes well.

Explore your reasons for being guarded. Undoubtedly, our body language and speech changes based on the interaction. How I communicate in a professional setting won't resemble the mannerisms I'll display at a cookout. But if you find it difficult to let your walls down, even in the company of your most intimate friends, there may be things you're not confronting. Safety with others should arise as a component of intimacy. Feeling safe enough to divulge who you are shouldn't be considered the same as an obligation to disclose information. Sometimes we are unaware of trust issues we may have with ourselves or others.

Although many may be unsuspecting, there are people who are well aware of the issues they have with trust. They can tell you the intricate details surrounding the moments of their trust-dissolving encounter. How does it affect your life when you make the decision to ignore it? Every situation we face must pass through the filters of our previous experiences. We decide what's good or bad based on having tried it on for size. A 5XL person simply cannot fit in a 1XL T-shirt.

Hoping to thrive in intimate relationships without confronting known trust issues, is like purchasing items of clothing you can't fit. There's no chance it will work out right.

Interrupt The Pattern

Change cannot occur without force. Something must disturb a pattern enough to alter it. Just because you're able to juggle the balls you have in the air, doesn't mean that's what you should be doing. Question why you do what you do, and decide if it fulfills you to continue. Unless it violates someone's safety, you are not obligated to continue what does not satisfy.

Deciding what to do next in any situation relies on your perception. How clearly are you seeing what's in front of you? It's peculiar how a group of people can witness the same event, but see it so differently. Our perspective has a voice and how we perceive things. Bob Dylan said, "Some people feel the rain, others just get wet." Purpose to be part of what's happening around you, and not just associated with it. In most cases, the clarity we need will come from angles we may not be in the correct position to see. Knowing you're in the right position to see what you need to, is a challenge within itself. We don't know what we don't know, until we finally come into the knowledge of it. Seeing bad things accumulating is much different than a perspective of them stacking up. With a system we can use strategies to manage any type of accumulation, but "stacking" has a negative connotation. Even in our thinking, we must keep all things at eye-level. When things are stacked, our tendency is to deal with what's on top first. You may never get to the root of the issue if it's consistently at the bottom of the pile. The point I'm making is, without seeing clearly, we can't be as objective as the situation demands. Some decisions are more sensitive than others, and require a different level of response. Uncomplicated matters don't always have to be as complicated as we make them. We've let our convenience trump our common sense. Why drive three miles to a corner store in a thunderstorm for a Mountain Dew and bubblegum? In this scenario, do the risks outweigh the wisdom of waiting for the storm to pass? We shouldn't live in fear of what could happen, but ignoring wisdom is irresponsible. The road is wet and slippery. It's difficult to see who or what's in front of you. And the likelihood of an accident increases during bad weather. Unless you have an addiction to fountain drinks and gum, the decision to wait and go later is a no-brainer.

Uncover The Gems

I enjoy watching home restoration shows. It's impressive how contractors can recapture the beauty of homes that have not been loved properly. There are certain things about houses that set them apart. A uniquely designed archway, or a full surround mantle can really draw attention to a room. A common practice amongst those who flip houses is to identify what's salvageable before the demolition begins. A big mistake rookie house-flippers make is to assume that entire rooms should be gutted. Some homes have gems that have been covered up for years. Experienced house rehabbers know how important it is to check underneath the carpet before destroying the floors. Every now and then they come across expensive hardwood floors that are still in excellent condition. When this happens, it's a savings of thousands of dollars.

How many times have we convinced ourselves that in order for us to be happy, we must completely start over? Like a well-crafted house, there's good in all of us. There may be several layers of debris, totally obscuring the view of what lies beneath, but the foundation is solid. Wheelbarrow by wheelbarrow, begin removing the rubble to expose your treasure.

Situations are sometimes more palatable when we change our outlook. Move from being a glass half empty person, to being someone who sees the glass as half full. We're talking about the same amount of water. There's nothing wrong with spinning things in a positive way. It's not lying. It's a reminder for the brain that hope is the best soil to nurture growth. I overheard a fascinating conversation two ladies were having about downsizing. One lady was sharing with the other about how she and her husband moved from their five-bedroom home, into a smaller two-bedroom home. She explained that their four kids were all grown and married with their own families now. In the old house, only the master bedroom was downstairs, and all of the kid's bedrooms were upstairs. Everything they needed was on the ground level, and neither her nor her husband had been upstairs in the last three years. The part that caused me to lean in was when she said, "My old house was larger, but I find that I enjoy my new house so much more. I walk in every room every day and it feels good knowing all the space I have has a purpose. I love the fact that nothing's being wasted". Who says the word downsize has to have a negative connotation?

Through whose eyes should I see things? Our perspectives are colored with bias. The expression, "seeing is believing", has a whole new connotation these days. Years ago, a photograph was concrete evidence that something actually happened. Today, not only still images can be digitally edited, but videos are also easily manipulated. Anyone with a cell phone has access to filters that can make a freak show of a person look like a goddess. Even without digital filters, we see things through the lens of our own experiences. But after establishing the validity of something being real, agreeing about what we see remains a challenge. The brutal police beating of Rodney King in 1991 had a polarizing effect on the world. People who felt constantly victimized by police saw the video one way, while those oblivious to that stigma saw it differently.

When people from different backgrounds, cultures, and experiences come together to discuss a topic, they bring unique insights and knowledge that others may not possess. This diversity of perspectives can shed light on various aspects of the topic that might have been overlooked or misunderstood.

Furthermore, different perspectives foster creativity and innovation. When individuals with diverse viewpoints collaborate, they can generate new ideas and solutions that might not emerge otherwise. By challenging each other's assumptions and beliefs, they can push the boundaries of what is known and explore new possibilities. Having diverse perspectives promotes critical thinking and intellectual growth. When people are exposed to viewpoints that differ from their own, they are forced to evaluate their own beliefs and opinions more critically. This process of reflection and analysis can lead to personal growth and a deeper understanding of oneself and the world around them.

Moreover, diverse perspectives foster not only empathy (as mentioned before), but also understanding. When individuals engage with others who have different backgrounds and experiences, they develop a greater appreciation for the complexities of the human experience. This can lead to increased compassion towards others, as well as a greater willingness to consider alternative viewpoints and experiences. Diversity of perspectives is essential for democracy and civic engagement. In a democratic society, it is important for people to have the opportunity to express their views and participate in public discourse. By ensuring that a wide range of perspectives is represented in decision-making processes, we can create more inclusive and equitable societies where everyone's voice is heard. Diverse perspectives can lead to better outcomes in various contexts, including business, education, and policymaking. Research has shown that diverse teams are more innovative, productive, and successful than homogeneous ones. By embracing diversity and inclusivity, organizations and institutions can harness the full potential of their members and achieve better results.

Dr. John D. McConnell

Hero Your Own Story

Being the hero of your own story is more than just a cliché; it's a profound truth that resonates with the human experience. At its core, being the hero means taking charge of your life, embracing challenges, and striving for growth and fulfillment. It's about recognizing your own agency and power to shape your destiny, regardless of the obstacles you may face.

Every person's journey is unique, with its own triumphs and trials. Being the hero of your own story means acknowledging that your life is an epic narrative, full of highs and lows, twists and turns. It's about owning your experiences, both good and bad, and using them to propel yourself forward. One of the key aspects of being the hero of your own story is taking responsibility for your actions and their consequences. This requires honesty with yourself, a willingness to learn from your mistakes, and a commitment to self-improvement. In every situation, the hero recognizes that they have the power to choose how to respond, and they strive to make choices that align with their values and goals.

Being the hero of your story also means embracing resilience in the face of adversity. Life is rarely smooth sailing, and every hero must weather storms along the way. Whether it's facing personal setbacks, navigating difficult relationships, or confronting external challenges, the hero perseveres with courage and determination. They draw strength from within, tapping into their inner resources to overcome obstacles and emerge stronger on the other side.

But being the hero isn't just about individual triumph; it's also about making a positive impact on the world around you.

Dr. John D. McConnell

Heroes are not passive bystanders; they are actively engaged in the world, seeking to make a difference in whatever way they can. This might mean standing up for justice, advocating for those who are marginalized, or simply spreading kindness and compassion in their daily interactions. This requires self-awareness and self-compassion. You should recognize your own worth and treat yourself with the same kindness and respect that you would extend to others. Exhale and be gentle with yourself when you fall short, celebrating your successes, and acknowledging your progress along the way.

At its heart, being the hero is about living authentically - embracing who you are, with all your strengths and weaknesses, and refusing to conform to others' expectations or ideals. The hero is unapologetically themselves, charting their own path and following their own truth, even in the face of opposition or doubt.

It doesn't mean going it alone. In fact, one of the hallmarks of a true hero is their ability to build meaningful connections with others. Heroes recognize the importance of community. They understand that asking for help is a recognition of shared humanity and interdependence. Even without having all the answers, we have the power to authentically show up, embracing our humanity, and striving to make the most of the precious gift of life. So go ahead, embrace your inner hero, and write the epic tale that is uniquely yours.

Dr. John D. McConnell

CHAPTER 5

TIME
ALLOTTED

I can't write a book about "time" without bragging on its résumé, at least a little. Time began fourteen billion years ago. About five thousand years ago, the Egyptians and Babylonians began measuring time to regulate cycles of planting and harvesting, to coordinate communal activities and public events, and to schedule the shipment of goods. They were responsible for the base twelve system we use to divide our days into twenty-four hours, and the base sixty system, for dividing each hour into sixty minutes. Throughout history people have recorded the passage of time using sunrise and sunset, and the phases of the moon. Time actually has no physical properties to measure. Conceptually, universal time is the rotation of the earth with respect to the sun. Earth revolves in orbit around the sun three hundred sixty-five days, six hours, and nine minutes.

 Dr. John D. McConnell

Man was not here when time began, and we had no voice in its occurrence. As we cannot change it, or make any adjustments to it, we can only operate in time. Let's learn as much as we can about it so that our interactions are sensible. Since we can't make time, let's purpose to make the most of it.

Our existence means nothing until we know why we are here. Our physical design, frailties, and tolerances all play a part in whatever we are to achieve. Methuselah, grandfather of Noah, had the longest lifespan of all those given in the Bible - living 969 years. Over the last century, no man is recorded to have lived beyond one hundred sixteen years. Why is that? Did the intention of our creator change? Or have we simply figured out how to get more done using less time? What we know for sure is, no one lives forever.

Every culture celebrates the birth of a

 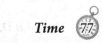

child differently, yet it is a celebration. From the moment we are aware of conception, the clock begins. Daily intentions have a much broader purpose because in an instant, we've moved from being 'the protected', to becoming 'the protector'. There is a life coming that we're totally responsible for. The success of your child's safety, nurturing, growth, and development becomes the mission that overshadows every other assignment we have. We have no idea who this child will grow to become, but that mystery does not dim our resolve. As we enter the world, so many questions go unanswered. Many of them will remain that way over our lifetime. For some of us, it becomes clear very early what we're passionate about. In most cases, passion is a prerequisite for purpose. Some stumbled onto their yellow-bricked road, while others claim to have never found that elusive shimmer at the end

 Dr. John D. McConnell

of the rainbow. I have always loved the poem by Linda Ellis, "The Dash". In it, she denotes the significance of the dash that sits between the date we were born, and the date our life ends. The poem contends that how we spend the time between those two dates, say more than any words we could utter.

Wild elephants typically live sixty to seventy years, and are important ecosystem engineers. Bats live about sixteen years on average, and are necessary for pest control, pollinating plants and dispersing seeds. Ducks are often found in wetlands, and as they move around to different wetland locations they introduce animal species, such as frogs or fish to new locations. Ducks live six to ten years. Most possums live five to eight years, and are beneficial for helping to control the overpopulation of snakes, rodents, and insects. We arrive at these connections through investigation.

However, only what is revealing and obvious floats to the surface. We will never know the full extent of our interdependence.

Whatever we are to accomplish, we've been rationed only a specific amount of time.

All of creation relies heavily upon what's already been done. In essence, we mimic what we see. Every species trains their offspring to be like them. The instinct to hunt, swim, climb, or fly may be innate, but seeing it modeled affirms the behavior. The way birds chirp and humans talk are all based on association. The movements of predators stalking their prey are learned from tutorials with mom and dad. Once what's inside us has an outlet for display, we begin seeing uncharacteristic new things occur. Life-changing inventions, amazing theories for learning, and cures for diseases are next to have a platform. It's inevitable that sparks of genius will brood out of the mundane. When faced with complacency, human ingenuity seeks to transform what is familiar into something illustrious. The part we represent in this genius transformation may be small, but definitely not insignificant. If your role is to encourage, motivate, and cheer, don't forsake your assignment. There is a season for all things, and we must be aggressive during the span of our influence.

The cycle of life dictates that all things come to an end after a period of time. Whether or not our usefulness has been maximized, there is an expiration. A loaf of bread, a vine of grapes, or a carton of milk, all have a limited amount of time as sources of nutrients. Even the greatest methods of preservation can't stop the inevitable from occurring. After several days, an abandoned banana will morph from yellow to liquefied black. Expiration stamps are helpful in that they remind us the end of effectiveness is drawing near. Consuming prescription medication after its expiration date will most likely not yield you the results advertised. The level of sophistication increases with humans. We obviously don't arrive with a placard detailing our purpose, or 'best used by' date. We don't know at what age we'll make our largest contribution to society. Never count yourself out. There's still lots of life to live after forty. At the age of forty-one, Donald Fisher and his wife opened their first Gap Store. When he was fifty, Leo Goodwin started the insurance company, Geico. Also at age fifty, Bernie Marcus co-founded Home Depot with a business partner. The day you lose hope and contemplate quitting could be the day before your largest triumph. Because you don't know, forfeiting can't be your solution. Also, because none of us know how much time we have, we dare not live as though time will never end.

 Dr. John D. McConnell

In our latter days, we'll begin to mourn what we considered our "best years". God, AKA Father Time, is 'the great equalizer'. Some people seem to have greater gifts, better opportunities, or more resources. We have friends who hit their target goals years before we hit ours. At times we feel we've been left at the starting block, far from being a contestant in life's race. We wonder why we have issues others aren't plagued by. Why is our road inundated with land mines? When will the burdens lighten and things become easier? Stories of our glory days include memories of being quicker, lighter on our feet, and more energetic. We remember being physically fit and anxious for activity. Being younger doesn't always equate to being better. We don't get to create the ranking, and sometimes what we must balance seems very unfair. For the most part, things have a way of equalizing. It's not that you're tracking those who seem to be ahead of you, but sometimes, when more of their story is revealed, you come to learn of their obstacles. No one makes it through life untouched by trouble. We could all maximize our strengths if we'd spend less time posturing and comparing.

It's easy to make excuses for why we aren't doing something now. In our mind, there is always a reason for justification. In many instances, the things we justify keep us pushing necessary decisions for change down the road. We postpone doing what we can now until it becomes something no longer within our ability to perform. I can have a goal to secure a commercial pilot's license, but if I never practice on a simulator, or do the coursework, it's to no avail. Depending on your goals, some expirations have already been set. The FAA enforces a rule that no commercial pilot beyond the age of sixty can pilot alone.

Manage your dreams effectively to prevent resentment. Because of expiration dates, there are rules that limit some of our dreams. It's poor goal management to decide at the age of fifty-nine that you want a commercial pilot's license. Since time is not reversible, we must employ organization in our execution.

Since a specific number of years have not been promised to us, we must forecast our longevity. It's on us to fix in our minds what we desire to accomplish by the end. Although there is no guarantee of completing the goals we've set, this type of forecasting gives us legitimacy. Until the true purpose of our life is revealed, something must hold its place. Even if it appears to others that we are living aimlessly, no one is completely without a target they're hoping to hit. Goals afford us direction and without direction, we drift. Drifting is far more hazardous than falling short of a goal. Goals have judgments connected to them. I had a Pastor who said this in a way that I'll never forget. Dr. Charles E. Perry, Jr said, "The judgment for leaving Houston, driving north on interstate 45 for 3 1/2 hours is Dallas". If you were missing, and the last person you spoke to knew of your goal to reach Dallas, Texas - this would streamline the search for you. If you're true to your goal, you should be found somewhere in the vicinity of the route to Dallas. On the other hand, an attempt to locate a drifter would be more chaotic. Having no expressed goal makes you more like a needle in a haystack to a search party. When we drift, we can unintentionally end up far from where we want to be. Some drift and never find a way back. Free will choices don't always offer round-trip itineraries.

You will never impact anyone more than those who have direct access to you. We are

Dr. John D. McConnell

inspired by characters celebrities portray in movies. We're drawn in and begin to identify with our favorite entertainers and public icons. However, we become fascinated with the idea of who they are. We don't actually know them. We can't testify to ever having watched them react to a real-life moment. The true champions of the world aren't on TV shows or on the field playing in Super Bowls. The original influencers are us. When I picture a man as a mentor for young boys, I see Thomas Womack. When I was a pre-teen, he sacrificed most of his Saturday mornings for the Junior Brotherhood at my church. When I picture an educational leader, I see Georgia Berry. She was my fourth-grade teacher, and the first school principal to hire me as an educator. When I picture a music mentor, I see Sharon Marshall. She was the first person to take me to a music recording studio at the age of sixteen. When I picture a true friend, I see Tracy Robinson-Stowers. We met in the 12th grade and never passed judgment upon each other. These names won't ring a bell with you, because according to the most popular definition of celebrity, they don't qualify. To me however, they're superstars. Likewise, you have the opportunity to reach celebrity status in the eyes of the people you interact with on a consistent basis. It can be difficult winning at life when we're fixated on legacy. Perhaps if we crop our focus to just today, tomorrow will begin to take care of itself. Your proximity to someone may only be months long. However, your season of influence could last their entire lifetime. Moments can become legendary, even without a legacy focus. After our lives are spent, we may not be known for what we hope to be known for. We may not even be remembered by a fraction of the people

 Dr. John D. McConnell

we meet. What I can guarantee is that we change the lives of the people we touch.

Making up for lost time is a universal concept that resonates with many people at different stages of their lives.

Understanding Lost Time

Lost time can take many forms. It may stem from procrastination, indecision, fear, or external circumstances beyond our control. People might feel they've wasted time on unfulfilling pursuits, failed relationships, or career choices that didn't align with their passions. Whatever the cause, the realization that time has slipped away can evoke feelings of regret, sadness, and frustration.

The Motivation to Make Up for Lost Time

The desire to make up for lost time often arises from a deep-seated longing for fulfillment and a sense of purpose. It can serve as a catalyst for change, spurring individuals to reassess their priorities, set new goals, and take decisive action. Whether it's pursuing a neglected passion, repairing damaged relationships, or advancing in a career, the motivation to reclaim lost time can fuel remarkable transformations.

Challenges and Obstacles

Making up for lost time is not without its challenges. Past mistakes and missed opportunities can cast a shadow of doubt and self-criticism, hindering progress, and causing anxiety about the future. Also, there may be practical obstacles such as financial constraints, limited resources, or external obligations that make it difficult to pursue new endeavors. Overcoming these hurdles requires a willingness to confront discomfort and uncertainty.

 Dr. John D. McConnell

Strategies for Moving Forward

To effectively make up for lost time, individuals must adopt a proactive mindset and embrace a growth-oriented approach to life. This involves:

1. **Setting Clear Goals**: Define specific, achievable objectives that align with your values and aspirations. Break them down into manageable steps to create a roadmap for progress.

2. **Taking Action**: Act decisively and consistently towards your goals, even if progress is incremental. Embrace a mindset of continuous learning and improvement, viewing setbacks as opportunities for growth rather than failures.

3. **Cultivating Resilience**: Develop resilience to navigate challenges and setbacks along the way. Embrace the

lessons learned from past experiences, using them as steppingstones towards a brighter future.

Experience Your Expectations

Psalms 118: 24 says, "This is the day the Lord has made. Let us rejoice and be glad in it".

Yesterday was the best day of my life! I hope to say the same thing about today, but it's only 6 AM. Yesterday was the best because I lived it that way. I got up early and did the things I wanted to do. I thought about things that were important to me, and actually did a bit of journaling. I spent my time and focus on what was good. I intentionally threw a smile at everyone I spoke to (in person and on the phone). Just like every day, I was baited with opportunities to be offended - but I didn't bite. I was deliberately positive in my interactions. I didn't rely on anyone or anything outside of myself for fulfillment. My expectations stay high - not for others, but for myself. I lived in the bonus part of life yesterday. A few things I had sown for arrived. You never know what day you'll reap what you've sown. The harvest always reflects what's been planted. Yesterday I made a choice to not dwell on what I couldn't do, or what I didn't have. I purposed to remain excited about the moment I was in.

Intuition, often described as a gut feeling or inner knowing, can be a powerful guide in decision-making. By tuning in to our intuition and listening to our inner voice, we can gain valuable insights into what we care about the most. Whether it's a sense of excitement, peace, or resonance, our intuition can help us discern between competing priorities and make choices that are in concert with our deepest desires.

CHAPTER 6

TIME USED

Time is very much like the words we say. Once we put them out there, we can never get them back. Our words can create, console, or inflict harm. Forgiveness for what you said may be an option, but you can never unsay it. Good or bad, whatever choices we've made with our use of time, can never be recouped. What's over, is over - and the best thing we can do is learn from it. It's of no real benefit to agonize over what you didn't get right. I challenge you to find a glint of optimism you can extract, no matter how bad your performance.

The city of Houston has had its share of tropical storms and hurricanes. Over several years, hundreds of lives have been lost due to the violent storms that frequent the Gulf of Mexico. With each threat, valuable data is accumulated that supports the city in its resilience campaign. Not many things prepare you better than personal experience.

The wisdom to survive a storm is valuable knowledge. It provides leadership to those who have not experienced your journey. Sports teams making a championship run, greatly benefit from having an experienced veteran in the locker room who's been part of a championship team. The cheer energy is different from those who've held the trophy. It's elevated from, "I believe we can do this", to "This is ours – let's take it"! What you've already gone through in life should be placed on a mantle and studied. The triumphs and failures of our past should greatly steer our future.

The first vehicle I owned was a used 1978 Datson pick-up truck. It was a five speed, banana yellow 620 series with a black leather bench seat. I was seventeen years old when my dad brought it home, and the only sibling interested in learning how to drive a stick shift. I didn't know where this truck had come from, or who owned it before me. The most important thing was that it was mine. I had no vehicle history, so I didn't know if it had been in an accident, or what if any roads outside of Kansas it had traveled. Perhaps it served its previous owner well. That's something I never investigated because I was too busy creating my own memories. The fact that it was a six-year-old used vehicle didn't concern me in the least. I was excited that it drove well and served as my chariot for my final two years of high school. The age of my vehicle was of no significance to the exploits and adventures accumulated during that season of my life. Those were moments of great value, and had they not happened the way they did, my life today would be different. Who I dated in 1983, what I drove in 1984, what college I attended in 1986, are all minor details when viewed separately. But when you connect all the minor details of your life, it's easy to see that every moment used was major and extremely consequential.

We trade the best of who we are for what's in our imagination. What we believe we will receive somehow is so much worth trading in what is valuable to us. I love the way Dr. Tony Evans laid it out during one of his sermons. As he talked about the Garden of Eden, he explained how Eve's attention was drawn away from all God said she had access to. Through the cunning of the serpent, she focused on the one tree He said she couldn't touch. Even with the promise of what we know we have; we are sometimes drawn away by lust or pride. I saw a movie starring Ben Affleck called Triple Frontier. An elite team of disbanded military specialists join together to take down a drug-lord. With the intel gathered, they efficiently planned their heist down to the smallest detail. Everyone had an assignment based on their expertise. Their synchronized attack was being executed perfectly until they realized there was a lot more money in the house than expected. Greed kicked in, and they abandoned their time clock to take millions more than they had originally planned. The collateral damage to the carefully planned op was significant. The extra time they took resulted in more lives being lost. The helicopter was rated for only a certain amount of weight, and because the engine started to fail, they were forced to throw millions of dollars over the side - and the helicopter still crashed. What we view as an epiphany, could be a damning distraction than unravels very well-laid plans.

Where we are today is a direct reflection of how we've used everything we've ever had. However we invest our thoughts, energy, money, or TIME, makes the needle move – but not always in the direction we hope for.

The great thing about our past is having a baseline we can compare other things to. Until we know what we don't like, our curiosity is like a mad scientist in a completely stocked laboratory. We treat life as an experiment, taking risks while trying to minimize loss. Although I feel risk should be a part of our lives, even in our golden years, the type of risks we entertain in our youth are much more precarious. The time we've used has already revealed our phobias, allergies, love-languages, and so much more. Make what you know about yourself a commodity. Use all of what you've learned to inspire and help others. No one is created exactly like us, but there are thousands who are very similar to us. There are people who live their entire lives, not knowing who they really are. They have blinders keeping them from seeing things that are so obvious to others. As you recognize yourself in the people you meet,

Dr. John D. McConnell

get intentional about having conversations. We grow through our willingness to share. I've heard it referred to as having a kindred spirit with someone. They seem so familiar – almost as if you had a twin sibling. When these types of relationships are nurtured, they become less one-sided. After a while, that kindred spirit you've been pouring into, may reveal something transformational you never expected to learn about yourself.

Morgan Freeman starred in a movie called 57 Seconds. He had a ring that harnessed the power to repeat the last 57 seconds. Everything and everyone responded to the actions of the bearer of the ring, no matter how many times those 57 seconds were reset. For me, that movie emphasized the importance of how we spend our time. Maybe we shouldn't measure our lives in years, months, and days. We must assign the right value to every minute of our lives.

How I treat you immediately affects the next person you interact with. Actions of love and hate have a domino effect, and we're all responsible for our part.

When my youngest son was in the fourth grade, I got him the bicycle he wanted for his birthday. It was a beautiful burnt orange color, and the bike chassis was a new elongated model. For the longest time he'd been wanting to ride a bike to school – now here was his moment. His mom and I got him a lock for his bike and explained the rules for protecting it. He was so excited to be in the "bike-rider group" for school dismissal, because they were the first group of students dismissed, allowing them to weave through the sea of vehicles awaiting car-riders. About three weeks into this new routine, Jadden rolls up to school, places his bike on the bike rack, but realizes he doesn't have his lock. Instead of riding back home and putting his bicycle in the garage, he elected to just go inside for a regular school day. He thought nothing of it all day, and when school let out, he was shocked that it was no longer there. Unfortunately, it was that day that opened my son's eyes to the dark side of people. He thought having a bike lock was to appease his mom and I, not knowing its purpose was to keep his bike from being stolen. It's irresponsible not to prepare your children for negative things you hope they won't face. How can we teach those lessons in ways that don't cause them to shut down? Things happen that change us forever. Some scars callous, while others heal with no visual blemish. Although people may never see the evidence of what we've endured, we live with what happened.

Six degrees of separation is the idea that all people are six or fewer social connections away from each other. No doubt we all have stories about the people we've met because of the people we know. It could be a friend of a friend's friend that affords you a very special opportunity. I don't believe in coincidence. It's my opinion that people generally end up where they're supposed to. I don't mean we're off the hook for the choices we make, but I believe we're ultimately responsible to step up in situations that bless others. Simply introducing someone or vouching as a reference is much different than putting your reputation on the line for someone. No matter our status in life, I believe we owe one another a hand up. When given an assist, manage your expectations. If someone famous invites you into their circle, it doesn't mean you will be famous. That type of thinking puts undue pressure on new relationships and can become the reason you can't walk together as friends. As you're building relationships, expect to cross

 Dr. John D. McConnell

paths with some really large personalities. Just like you, famous people are looking to connect with people who won't manipulate or use them.

Is disengaging the same as letting go? Time has revealed to me that they are two separate things. I've had the intent to let go of situations that later became blessings in my life. It's not always that we need to totally abandon a pursuit. We reach intersections in our lives, where we must take a hard pause. We're not necessarily ready to throw it away, but we realize we can't continue the path the same way. This is when we disengage. It's healthy to take a step back and get a good gaze at where you are. God himself did so as He was creating our world. He stopped, not only to admire, but also to evaluate His work. He didn't reengage until He agreed with Himself, that it was good. As time matures, perspectives and circumstances sometimes make re-engaging an excellent choice.

We grow bigger than many situations we're connected to. This is when we must let go. Have you ever tried letting go of something that wouldn't let go of you? Allowing things and people to occupy spaces in your life that no longer serve a purpose, delays what's next from entering. Holding on to what no longer fits, creates regret, and we already have enough of that.

The reference point of life must be the sovereignty of God. The sovereignty of God says that things are under control when they're out of control. Life always feels like chaos when it doesn't fit inside the frame we try to put it in. Being comfortable with where we are in life has much to do with being in sync with what's happening. If every step I took required complete understanding and no hesitation, I'd never move. Usually the confidence I have in making decisions comes from how things worked out the last time. With enough repetition, we learn that we must trust the process. It's scary to admit that our answer to some questions is, "I don't know". Here is an oxymoron for you. Get comfortable with being uncomfortable. You're not in charge anyway.

Everything we posture ourselves against isn't meant to destroy us. But it's hard not to be threatened by things we don't see as beneficial. Patience and time deal with things in a way that prevent us from ever having to lift a finger. I am grateful to those who blazed trails ahead of me. In all walks of life, many battles were fought, excusing me from having to step into a combat zone. Doors once closed to me are now open. Ironically, some things that used to be highly accessible have been stripped away. As time trends, we must keep our eyes on the wins and losses. Although change is inevitable, all change isn't good change. There will always be battles to fight, just new ones.

The place we call home guards our most intimate secrets. It's our retreat at the end of a long day. It's not only where we take off our proverbial masks, but we literally unrobe there. Home is where we exhale and disregard our posture. It's our place of vulnerability, solace, and refuge. No place is more comfortable or private than where we lay our heads at night. The house you live in doesn't care how you became the occupant, nor whether you were the first or the fourth to move in. With time it earns your trust of intimacy and safety. In the shower, we wash off the dirt and grime from our day, while singing a little song to celebrate the day's completion. While standing in the mirror brushing our teeth, we give ourselves a peptalk about how well we did today, and

Dr. John D. McConnell

how much better things will be tomorrow. As we prep meals in the kitchen, we role-play conversations we plan to have the next day at work. Dinner time has laughter and stories about everyone's day.

And when we enter the bedroom and lay down at night, we experience sweet sleep and beautiful dreams. Home is the gym that fortifies and conditions our mental stability. According to the US Census Bureau, the average American will have eleven different residences in their lifetime. Think about every place you've lived. Growth will always require change, and some changes occasionally demand you work out at a new gym. Make every place you live your home, and when you leave to occupy another one, take only the fondest memories.

Everything we'll ever do matters. We remember a lot of it, but probably forget just as much. The parts we forget aren't less important– just missing. Have you ever tried to put a puzzle together that was missing pieces? It's not until you realize too many being gone, render the puzzle unsolvable. Sure, there are memories we've suppressed because of seasons of trauma, but that was then. Perhaps the older you (mature, more experienced, more adaptable) can place that trauma in a perspective that fosters healing. I'm not challenging you to dig up what you've buried. I'm suggesting that what happened can now become your power. Not everything we fail to remember was traumatic for us. We tend to forget things we don't categorize as being relevant. Even now, forty years later, my younger brother is sharing details of memories that greatly impacted him, that I was unaware of at the time. I was there, but I guess it wasn't as significant to me. The awesome part of this is that I still have an opportunity – not to justify my actions, but

 Dr. John D. McConnell

to validate his feelings. It's not always about us. Stepping up to be a reliable person has no statute of limitations. We focus so much on our actions, that sometimes we overlook moments when we choose to do nothing. Everything we'll ever do, or elect not to, matters!

Like the paint on the exterior of a house, things lose their appeal with time. If it's been difficult to live beyond some devastating occurrences, keep living. Time erases the bold outlines of our past. Eventually, old news becomes just that - outdated, unpopular, and uninteresting. If something negative defined you years ago, your patience will reward you a new opportunity to redefine yourself.

When other factors partner with time, we have an opportunity to see just how powerful time can be. Water constantly flowing over or under the surface of concrete causes the sub material to wash away, leaving voids and settling concrete. Geologists debate the age of the Grand Canyon to be five to seventy million years old. Over the years, the Colorado River cut through the Colorado Plateau, carving out what we now call the Grand Canyon. Positive actions coupled with time may allow you to outlive the rough draft of your life. Use today to work on your edits and revisions and remain hopeful for things getting better.

Dr. John D. McConnell

CHAPTER 7

TIME
AVAILABLE

What will you do with the time you have left? The beautiful part about planning a future is being able to draw from the past. To minimize repeating mistakes we've already made, we must create a more intentional roadmap. On the surface, it appears that I have less – less time, energy, and youth. But in reality I have much more wisdom, intention, and purpose. Getting things right at this point feels more critical because an older you becomes interested in legacy. In order to leave something behind for the people we love, we must begin to create it. Whether it's a legacy of finance, business, or integrity. we realize in our older age that time is running out. Ask a teenager and a senior citizen what maximizing time means, and you'll get two totally different answers. Even with the very best time management practices, there's no way a teenager understands what maximizing time means.

Dr. John D. McConnell

They can comprehend what equates to being the best use of their time, but maximizing it is something that only comes with age. Unless or until you can sense the end of your life approaching, it's my opinion that one can't fully know what it means to maximize their days. Maximizing time has a further reach than just how you spend it. It involves your feelings which dictate the why, when, and how.

Although it's quite normal to develop a sense of urgency when we feel our time is running out, there is grieving for the things we've never made time for. I hear stories all the time about people who die days before retiring from the workforce. We witness people put gratification on their calendar, but never get to redeem the voucher. It's imperative we realize that life is to be enjoyed. Being financially responsible doesn't mean you must always delay self-gratification.

Actually, finding the balance between work and play, extends our mental and physical acuity. Timely vacations allow us to reset and refocus.

There comes a time in our adult years when we learn to have more of an appreciation for time. From our lists of what has gone right and what has gone wrong. it's easier to see the time we have left as a blessing. Some of our battles scars run deeper than others. We have handicaps that force us to approach things differently. Getting to our destined place may be more tedious because of new obstacles, yet we are still present and accounted for. Everyone's journey isn't allowed an extension, but we are still in the hunt. That alone is a blessing.

I have found that it is easy to miss moments. Have you ever experienced yourself making connections for things that have already passed? It's almost like being

Dr. John D. McConnell

out of sync with your thoughts. Have you ever had a great idea for a gift for someone immediately after their big celebration? I believe those things happen more than we realize. Perhaps we're treating every day as moments we should react to, rather than moments we should guide. Of course we can't make the future, but we can certainly become more interactive concerning it. It's become common place to complain about things that have already happened. Are we willing to accept a more hands-on role regarding what's next?

I recently went on a cruise with my sister. The cruise line offers a check-in process two weeks prior to each cruise that allows you to inform them of any special needs you may have. I always make them aware of my low vision. Upon boarding the ship during in-person check-in, again I was asked if I had any special needs they could assist with during the cruise. As if for the first time, again I made them aware of my low vision. The check-in attendant informed me that they could print a schedule of the onboard activities in large print and make them available each day of the cruise for me. I told them I'd greatly appreciate that accommodation. The cruise began Monday, but my first printout of activities did not arrive at my cabin until Wednesday morning. It seemed to irritate my sister more than it bothered me. She said that companies like to gesture to offer amenities for people with special needs, but fall short in actually delivering the service in an excellent way. I think I didn't show my irritation with their tardiness because I've grown accustomed to that type of disappointment. Even after receiving the printed activities in larger font, it was still too small and not legible for me. My sister felt I had a responsibility to complain. "John", she said, "unless they know there's a problem, nothing will change". She suggested that perhaps the cruise line could benefit from me being a consultant to assist them with establishing a better focus to actually meet needs of people with vision impairments. I think that's a great idea, and it forced me to confront my acceptance of empty gestures towards my disability. I must affect the change I want to see in the world, or else I'm lending myself to the problems and not the solutions. You must affect your world in that same way regarding the things that affect your life and members of your community. The time we have is not simply our own. Our voices can empower so many.

Although we've never been in charge of how much time we actually have here on earth, the clock seems to tick louder as we age. In our fifties, we realize we probably have less days remaining than the number of days we've already lived. It isn't an unsettling fact, but definitely one you can't ignore. While we are trying to become the change we want to see in the world, we must also figure out how to put ourselves first. If you're even remotely like me, over the years, you've divided yourself into so many different pieces, you're far from being whole. Our children have a slice, as well as our jobs, friends, church, etc.. Before there is only a shell of ourselves remaining, we must learn to become selfish. After twenty-nine years of marriage, I discovered in divorce that I had lost touch with who I was as an individual. That's not to say I was unhappy, but I was clearly compartmentalizing myself. When we're spread too thin, we don't always realize the parts we've given away. There is an expression that says, "as long as people are in my debt, I'll never be broke". It's time to call in your chips. If you're ever going to live for you, it must begin today. Prioritizing our personal needs actually makes us better givers. Becoming self-actualized is a gift that continues to give. When we learn of opportunities to have and do better, it's instinctive to share that information with as many people as we can.

Let's call this our 'now time'. Now is when we stop ignoring what our body has been telling us it needs. Now is when we give ourselves permission to take naps in the middle of the day. It's when we take long walks, not strictly for exercise, but for mental clarity. Now is when we recognize fast food as the enemy, and choose healthy garden salads to extend our days. Make choices today that help ensure a prosperous tomorrow.

Lock Your Expectations

Make specific plans for only what you expect to see in your life. Too many things have already shown up in our lives at random. With the time we have left, we can't waste energy and plans for things we are not really confident we can bring into our life. Choose goals you know you can conquer and begin stacking your victories. Fulfilled expectations improve happiness - and joy is strength.

Once you realize where you stand concerning certain people, use that to your advantage. We get a strong sense of people when we spend quality time around them. Don't turn off your senses. It can take years to find people you really connect with, so when you find a connection that's real, embrace it. Avoid the mistake of not letting people know their presence in your life is impactful. When we feed our relationships with necessary fuel, they get hotter and produce so much more. People will give more of themselves when they know it's appreciated. It's not manipulation if it's genuine. We're always in a defensive posture, trying to distinguish what's real from what's fake. Unfortunately, there are always deceivers on the prowl. But when you do find personalities that lock with yours, be intentional not to take them for granted. Iron sharpens iron, and we all need people around us who make us better. Making mistakes in relationships is a part of life. There will always be unavoidable collateral damage if your purpose is to win in friendship. To get the best from any relationship, you must surrender to it. That vulnerability offers direct access to your heart, and that's always a risky proposition. But the alternative is to remain guarded. Being protective of your heart, goals, dreams, thoughts, and feelings is normal - but finding someone safe to open up to will allow growth to become exponential. There is a freedom in being able to openly release who we are.

When our release meets validation, who we are increases in volume. Disastrously I've hurt people without the intention of doing so. My response used to be to never try again, until I realized the best way forward isn't isolation, but total honesty.

I recently heard someone say, "Regret for time wasted is more time wasted". It's a terrible feeling to know when someone is wasting your time, and you can do nothing about it. It's inevitable that we'll accept an invitation to a party we're not really interested to attend, or have dinner with business associates we don't care for. The last thing I want to do after those moments are over, is reboot a conversation about it, essentially living it all again. Learn to interrupt moments of waste. It's your time, and if you don't place value on it, no one else will. If you don't develop strategies to contain the time you're leaking, expect to continue to live with regret. Business consultant, Myron Golden says he never flies commercial. Commercial airlines require passengers to arrive two hours prior to their flight time (outbound and returning). He explains that, although it financially costs him more to fly private, he's willing to pay for the convenience of his time not being wasted. We don't have to all agree on the same strategies for maximizing time, but once we identify the leaks, we must plug the holes. Unless you become inspired to regard time more reverently, you'll finish everything you start. That's not always a good thing. Some things we start don't qualify for a finish. I'm not going to finish a meal that tastes horrible just because I ordered it. If the rear speakers in the movie theater noticeably stop working, I shouldn't have to suffer through a movie I purchased to see and hear in Dolby surround sound. I'm living for magical moments now instead of the regular routine. Experiencing life at its highest level requires us to be ready to advocate for ourselves at all times. That's something you should never have to apologize for.

For some odd reason, there is an expectation for us to pay more for what should be included as a basic service. It's called a convenience fee. To pay a bill over the phone may cost you more than mailing a check. Why is that? It seems to me the company receiving the phone payment is conveniently getting paid instantly. Nothing could be more convenient. We pay more for the things we don't question. I think we don't ask as many questions today because we've grown satisfied with saving time. In some circles, saving time means more than saving money. Think about that for a moment. The washing machine, dryer, dishwasher, and microwave were all created because of our compulsion to save time. It's not a new concept, but it seems we're paying even more these days. This suggests that people are more confident in their ability to earn money than they are in being able to replace time. Where do you stand? Are you being left back in the era of the clothing line – hoping for a mild warm breeze to dry your garments? You obviously must come into your own decision, but time is definitely not a renewable resource. I don't believe there is a limit to how much we'll pay for more time. Whether it's money, sweat equity, or bartering, we will pay it if it's ours to give. Some cancer patients and organ transplant recipients have medical bills that exceed five hundred thousand dollars, but being alive will always trump time served. How do you make your time worth more to you today than it's ever been worth before?

We must live well enough long enough to become comfortable with the idea of dying.

I've heard people say they're ready, but I've not met many comfortable with making the transition. It is very possible to find peace with death, but not before you're fulfilled with living. Do you see sunrises, or do you simply notice the sun is shining? Do you witness sunsets, or do you only notice the sun has gone down? There is a difference, and it's vast. Once you grow from noticing moments to experiencing moments, life offers new perspectives. It's impossible to live your best life if you've never seen it from the right view. The perspective I'm speaking of can't be taught. It's an appreciation the soul captures.

When we reflect upon the most impactful happenings of our lives, we judge them based on where we are now. Who we were back then is a blur. We remember what happened and the roles we played, but the strings that guided us then are no longer attached. In

 128 *Dr. John D. McConnell*

fact, many of us are unrecognizable as who we were before. Much of what we have today (debt, sickness, divorce, etc.) is because of how we lived then. Even the behaviors we want to forget will forever be part of our documented record. Essentially we've set ourselves up for this very moment. Fortunately, life moves in cycles. Just like we set ourselves up for now, we can use what we know to set ourselves up for the time that remains. Use the wisdom from everything you did that caused damage, to repair and improve your standards for life. If you were strong-armed before, by a force you could not overpower, now is the time to retaliate. Make your life reflect the beauty and strength you've always been aware of. Allow your hunger for life's zest to become your new puppeteer. Vow to not only be present for every moment, but to fully participate.

Moving forward sometimes requires

looking back. It may be difficult to own some things we've done, but experiencing true freedom may rely on your connection with others. Perhaps there is an apology we need to make, or a debt that's gone unpaid. Not everything we ignore erodes with time. Big things fester and callous. Responsibly owning your part may play a significant role in restoring the life of someone you hurt. It may also be the very thing that sets you free.

CHAPTER 8

INTENTION

"We judge ourselves by our good intentions, but we are judged by our last worst act" (*Michael Josephson*).

Following most big blowouts, I hear the phrase, "It wasn't my intention" mentioned a lot. It almost seems that for many people, just as much happens outside of our intention as the things we actually purpose to do. Could the reason be because perhaps we're not as intentional as we believe we are? The majority of us know what we don't want, but locking in on true desires is somewhat hit or miss. There are always reasons for the things we do. We eat when we're hungry and drink when we're thirsty. Those are foundational reasons. We also know people who eat and drink when they're not hungry or thirsty. We apply theories such as excessive brain endorphins, or emotional eating, but something is working as a trigger. The how and why questions in life are difficult

Dr. John D. McConnell

because the answers are forever changing. Ones reason for wanting a divorce can be the same reason they once desired marriage. It's chaotic but true. We are continuously evolving and the truth is, we don't always know what we want. I'm not trying to paint a picture of an irrational person with a fear of commitment. I'm simply validating that aloofness we've all experienced. When someone tells you what they want or why they're saying or doing a certain thing, it's because they believe it's true. Just know that what's true of them today may not be true of them tomorrow.

I have a friend whose mom and dad are surgeons. Their parents were surgeons as well. My friend has an older brother and sister who both elected different specialties, yet are surgeons. No doubt, the expectation for Tien to become a surgeon has always been overwhelming. It never felt like a daunting task she had to live up to, but more like a mantle or birthright. The way Tien has lived her entire life has been steered by her intention to become a surgeon. After successfully graduating from medical school, she was overcome with a desire to not be a surgeon, but a public-school teacher.

Allow your intentions of today to drive your actions. Stay in tune with what you want and where you're headed. Understand that it's okay to change your mind; however, it looks and feels better when you know you've shifted before others point it out to you. If you're confused by where you are in life, maybe you're still trying to give life to old intentions.

What if your mind changes but you don't?

The people who've spent the most time around us believe they know us the best. Although that's usually the case, game shows become popular from this ambiguity. Just because you think you know someone doesn't mean you really know them at all. In most cases, who we become closely correlates to how we've been raised - but even that's not a perfect science. One plus one does not always equal two. What makes intention so powerful is that usually it is the most pressing thing on your mind. If being an outstanding parent and excellent spouse are strong convictions for you, those things stay at the forefront of your thinking. When our motives are based on intention, there's an intrinsic motivation. A pat on the back isn't required when I'm already sold on the vision.

With the same potency of positive intentions standing at the ready, negative intentions await our command. There may be people who've caused you harm who you don't want to succeed. If you're secretly harboring malicious thoughts towards someone, the power of intention will unmask your façade.

Intention alone is not enough to make the abstract concrete. I can very much want to stick to my diet and exercise plan to lose twenty pounds, but what if the forces aligned against my desires are just as intentional? What about factors that affect weight - like genetics, cultural background, and mental health? There are also medical conditions such as hypothyroidism, sleep apnea, and PCOS that can wage a battle against weight loss. Although my intention is clear, these things, which can affect appetite and motivation to shop and cook healthy food or be active, stand just as resolute.

Organ transplant recipients can attest to the rigor involved in forcing your body to do something it wasn't designed to do. Since we're not born with a transplanted organ, the body will try to reject the unfamiliar body part. Immunosuppressants have been engineered to help the body prevent rejection. What I'm hoping to make clear is that intentionality, no matter how strong, is only one step towards bringing our desires into our embrace. Although extremely important, our intentions cannot override systems as ironclad as gravity. Our will must work in conjunction with the laws of nature and physics. This doesn't mean there aren't people who have more advantages. Unfortunately, whenever there is human interaction, there is a potential for manipulation. Having the best intentions does not guarantee yours to be favored. It's good to have positive intentions to remind us of our goals. Life has a way of beating us into submission unlike we've ever imagined. Even after devoting many years to a singular focus, the devastation of an unrealized dream can be our reward. When your dreams do not manifest, your intentions must remain strong. Motivational messages major in echoing that your dreams will come true. If you were dreaming the right way, with shameless boldness, you may not see them all come to fruition. But let it never be said that you were not intentional in doing your part. We make our plans, not knowing how long we'll be interested in the object of our affection. Going full throttle is sometimes difficult because we question our own sketchy track record. If we could be distracted before, what's to keep it from happening again? It's normal to have feelings of doubt. Doubt is a natural human emotion, and it is something that everyone experiences in their lifetime. What matters most is how you fight it, and whether you let it affect your life.

For many of us, doubt was a seed planted early in life. My family and pretty much all of those we associated with, were well

 Dr. John D. McConnell

acquainted with struggle. Going to church was like unplugging from real life, and temporarily plugging into a charging station. My church was interactive. We shouted back what was shouted at us from the pulpit - almost as though we were fighting to actually believe what we were saying. We doubted ourselves and our community's ability to support its own programs. As a kid, I didn't feel that we truly believed in ourselves, but solely in the power of God. "God's gonna make everything all right. The Lord will put food on our table and make sure our bills are paid." When you grow up doubting that you have skills that matter, it becomes something you must battle to unlearn as an adult.

You must respect the things you fear. Our preparation becomes heightened when we respect our fear as a worthy opponent. We must be intentional regarding things and people we perceive as a danger to us.

Our actions and the things we say can bring them closer or push them further away. I learned as a kid that to hide from a bully is no defense at all. Avoidance becomes a pattern that perpetuates more and more compromise. We must intentionally stand up and face what has us fearful. Once we respect the power it's wielding over us, we can begin to take it back. One of the questions you're asked when you join a fitness center is, "What are your goals?" Even if your goal is as singular as losing weight, nothing can be singular about your plan. The strategies you choose to incorporate must respect the problems you've been having with weight control. If the issues for the problems are never dealt with effectively, they will remain. Not only will they remain; they will grow. Intention supports us in starving our fears of what they've been using as fuel to overtake us. Triumphs are not a fluke. Pay attention

Dr. John D. McConnell

to them all because winning isn't a random thing. Something you did or said caused you to get that win. You want to know so it will repeat. There was a Christmas movie I watched a while back featuring Danny Glover. In the movie, his wife of many years had passed, and he was longing for a sweet-potato pie she used to make. Her book of recipes was in the kitchen, but he could not locate the recipe for the pie. Every day for two weeks, he made a new pie, trying to duplicate the taste of his wife's sweet-potato pie. He was intentional to write down every ingredient with each try just in case he got it right. Every time he got close, he'd alter an ingredient or measurement, and things would go the other way. By the end of the movie, shockingly, he got it right on Christmas Day. Sometimes if we are willing to mix our intentions with repetition, we'll get the desired result. What's the worst thing that could happen? Persistence puts us on the path towards excellence. We can all use a good story to tell.

How do you end up with what you don't want? When we let our proverbial guard down, anything is likely to show up. Success in life is not only based on what you're intentional about bringing to you. Don't make the mistake and forget that there is an attraction about you. I use lots of movie references because I love them so much. In the movie, "I Am Legend", Will Smith's character had to be extremely careful to use ammonia or bleach to hide his scent on his way home each night. Although the zombies in the movie could not come out in sunlight, at night, like a shark in the water, they could almost taste the blood they smelled in the air. As you're learning to seize the day to gain more, sure up your defenses. I've heard the expression, "for every level there is a new devil". It means there are some things you never have to deal with unless or until you reach the level where those things are. For instance, the rules of your checking account may impose a maximum daily withdrawal limit of two thousand dollars, but you've never had more than one thousand dollars in your account. You won't be affected by that rule until you have more money at your disposal. Some banks also have a maximum deposit limit. If this is news to you, it proves my point – "new levels, new devils". While you're figuring out how to add to your life, there are others working just as hard to take it all away. The majority of us are well-versed in staying beneath the radar. Most eyes aren't on us for living the common life. Our opinions can't really get us in trouble if we don't have an audience paying attention to what we're saying. That's a freedom that can always shift as you gain more notoriety in the world. Intentionally prepare for it all.

About seven thousand new species are found each year and there are more than one million different kinds of insects known in the world. Entomologists estimate there may be as many as ten million undiscovered insect species. I'll never understand those who refuse to acknowledge that there is a God. They give science credit for creation, while science (at best) can only try to explain what already exists based on discovery. Science knowledge will always be open to questions and revisions as we ascertain new evidence, causing us to postulate new ideas. As we think about the creation of our planet, let's focus on "the why". Anything created begins with intention. It's when we can't fully comprehend the intention of a thing that we misappropriate it.

Dung Beatles are very unsavory insects;

however, they play an important and remarkable role. While they feed on manure and use it to provide housing and food for their young, they improve nutrient recycling and soil structure.

Don't isolate your focus upon the dung beetle's intention. Zoom out wider and consider his creator's intention. We're cogs in the machine of life. Without you being functional, everything gets thrown off balance. Recognize your role, but never overestimate it. I'd never call a reader a dung beetle, but the comparison I'm making is - the role of each is just as vital for sustaining life.

Your being created was intentional. No matter the circumstances surrounding your birth, you were not a mistake. We all have a story, and yours may be plagued with turmoil. But the very fact that you are here supports your legitimacy.

Being fully functional as a valuable contributor demands that we walk in acceptance of who we are. Your worth is immense, and until you realize it, you'll diminish the potency of your privilege. Our scars qualify us for the resilience our purpose requires. Perhaps many people can do what you do, but not the way you do it. You can be substituted, but replacing you is impossible. It's because of your story that you relate to others the way you do. You feel what you feel because of where you've been. Who you're meant to affect in the world has been predetermined. The paths for those meaningful encounters will intersect at the appropriate time. That's not the part you can control. The best gift we could ever give ourselves is to fall in love with who we are. Unanswered questions will always be part of our composition, but the ability to push forward despite what we don't know is the key. Amazingly, some gaps are filled in along the way. They won't be answers we find, but revelations we discover. There is a place of freedom we must aspire to. Some think freedom is being able to answer all the questions that had us baffled. Freedom for a woman who's been confused is peace. Freedom for a man who's never been able to pay his bills, is being able to pay his bills. It will not look the same for you as it does for me. Once we begin to walk in our freedom, we gain the liberty to become pliable to our destined intentions.

In baseball, the pitcher is always looking to get the ball over home plate. The game of basketball is pointless without getting the ball in the hoop. The net is the aim of every soccer player. And every field goal kicker in football dreams of kicking the ball through the goalposts to win the game at the end of regulation. As in sports, success in most anything requires aim.

I have aimed and missed more targets than I cared to discuss. Repeatedly missing your mark is tough, and it can easily cause one to identify as a failure. Many people just surrender. With each missed shot, the big, colorful dreams are gradually reduced to a series of safe lateral movements. That's no way to capture joy and fulfillment.

Surely you didn't think I'd end this chapter without a resolve. I've stumbled onto a path that rewards me for every shot I take. The problem has not been my aim, but my target. Sometimes the goals we're trying to hit are too small. Imagine trying to get a fifty-inch beachball into a thirty-inch basketball hoop. No matter how many shots you take, the ball will never pass through. I believe our decisions for formulating our goals are flawed. By whatever method we use, we finalize our goal with locked-in coordinates. I contend that the expectations we place on our goals are too specific. The aim is important, but the journey is most vital. Along the way to our fixed coordinates, so many things in our lives will shift.

I saw a movie about a guy desperately trying to get to the woman he loved. Flights were canceled due to bad weather, and many stranded passengers in the airport were scrambling to make alternative travel arrangements. By chance, a woman ahead of him in the rental car line, secured the last vehicle available. After discovering they're both headed in the same direction, they agree to make the drive together. Neither of them aborted their intention of reaching the destination city, but so many things happened along the way to complicate the primary goal. By the time these two made it to their destination, their hearts had joined together - totally disrupting the original plan. Setting goals gets us on the right road, but remaining open to the target our arrow actually hits, could result in a better outcome. If we remain flexible, perhaps we'll see missed targets as alternative possibilities. Don't reduce the size of your dreams. Expand your tolerance for outcomes you've not considered.

While spontaneity can be exciting, having a well-thought-out plan provides direction, purpose, and a roadmap to success. Steering where you'd like to go is crucial in navigating the complexities of life and achieving desired goals. Here's why having a plan is better than having no plan at all. With a desired target in mind, you know exactly what you're working towards and can channel your efforts more effectively. Structuring the path allows you to allocate resources efficiently. Whether it's time, money, or manpower, having a plan helps prioritize where and how resources should be utilized to maximize productivity and minimize waste.

Dr. John D. McConnell

Risk Management

Planning with intention involves anticipating potential obstacles and devising strategies to overcome them. By identifying risks in advance, you can develop contingency plans to mitigate their impact, increasing your chances of success even in challenging circumstances. An outline serves as a benchmark against which you can measure your progress. It provides a framework for monitoring milestones and evaluating whether you're on track to achieve your objectives. This feedback loop enables you to make necessary adjustments and course corrections along the way. Having actionable strategies gives you something to strive for and helps maintain focus amidst distractions. When you know what you're working towards and why it matters, it's easier to stay galvanized and overcome obstacles that may arise. By breaking down larger goals into smaller, manageable tasks with deadlines, you can prioritize your activities and avoid prolonged stalls. This disciplined approach to time management allows you to make steady progress towards your intentions. When you have a clear plan in place, you're more likely to recognize and capitalize on opportunities as they arise, rather than letting them pass by unnoticed. While having a plan is important, it's equally essential to remain adaptable and flexible. Circumstances change all the time, and unexpected hurdles may arise along the way. A well-designed plan allows for flexibility and adaptation, enabling you to adjust your approach as needed without losing sight of where you're really trying to go.

Dr. John D. McConnell

CHAPTERR 9

FACING YOUR
FEARS

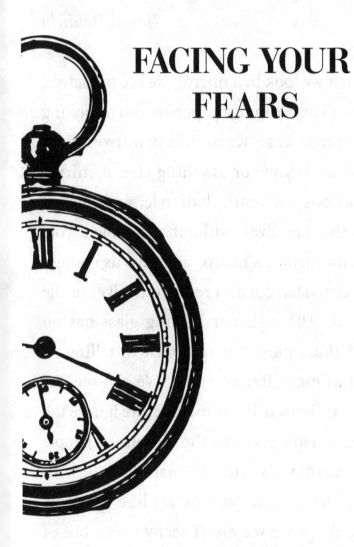

"Not everything that is faced can be changed, but nothing can be changed until it is faced."

-James Baldwin

When we look in a mirror, we see ourselves. There's no escaping the person you're looking at. In most cases we confide in mirrors more so than anyone or anything else. A mirror sanctions the outfit, hairstyle, and lipstick for the day. Even without a complete vote of confidence, a mirror can give us enough peace to step out and reveal ourselves to the world. Although our looking glass has no verbal abilities, it is complicit in telling us just as many lies as truths. We can see our total reflection, but sometimes we ignore the angles. How else can the billions of people on earth walk outside their homes with confidence each day? We act like the dents and dings we see aren't really there, but of course, that doesn't make them go away.

Dr. John D. McConnell

We can use make up and wardrobe tricks to hide - but unlike an automobile, we can't always buff things out.

The opportunity to confront who we really are is always available. Being true to ourselves can be awkward and difficult. At times it means we must admit to our fears. It's challenging to confess to something you don't fully understand. We realize we have trouble facing situations, but we might not know exactly why. It's not uncommon to go several years without addressing the 'elephant in the room'. We'll expend additional energy to prevent confronting the obvious antagonist. What if we could amass the right amount of courage to actually face our fears? We've lost so much time evading what's been staring us in the face. Think about how much better the quality of your life could be on the other side of your obstacle. You might find a whole new you just by stepping up to the challenge.

There's no way to know how many versions of you are locked behind one primary fear. Flooding light into those dark areas force the other hidden parts of you to be set free. You have no way of knowing what true freedom is until you've comprehensively dealt with your bondage.

AGITATION

What is the source of your agitation? Fear is not the only emotion that slows us down and throws us off our game. If we investigate our roots, we can make the connections for why certain scenarios cause us frustration. Somewhere along your journey, someone said or did something that had a profound negative effect. Perhaps you witnessed something paralyzing, or overheard a cruel intention. You may have even played a role in something horrific. The desire to cross the street when we perceive a familiar dread

 Dr. John D. McConnell

approaching is understandable. I fully support tabling troubling situations. We all have stories we can tell of things we should have disengaged from for a length of time. The right perspective sometimes is only revealed after disconnecting.

The fear, agitation, or frustration becomes something much larger when we allow it to sit on the shelf too long. As years go by, we perfect the art of transference. This is when we assign a whole new meaning to situations that may be totally unrelated to the truth. At this point, tabling the matter has shifted from coping strategy to fiction. To never attempt to work through why you're fearful, takes all of the power away from you and places it in the hands of your foe.

It's not unheard of to become afraid of who you believe you've become. As we pay attention to our track record, we might not be happy with the patterns we notice. I'm not always satisfied with myself, and sometimes I'm shocked by what those close to me say about my behavior. Deep down I think we all would like to be able to justify every decision we've made. The truth is, we're going to get it wrong sometimes. That's part of the human condition. Accountability is an important part of being a responsible person. Those who aren't accountable to anyone most likely get low grades in the court of public opinion. It's hard to make improvements when you can't identify your weaknesses. When you're overwhelmed with life, it's not always easy to recognize when you're losing ground. As a supervisor, it's challenging to hear that your leadership style causes people to not want to work hard for you. Just because you don't notice it, doesn't make it untrue. That's never the type of feedback you're eager to hear, but wouldn't you want to know while there's still a chance to improve your team's morale?

Dr. John D. McConnell

It's uncanny how much we can closely resemble members of our family. Not only our physical characteristics, but our mannerisms can twin our parents. That's a compliment for most people, but for those who grew up terrified or abused by family, sharing anything in common feels like a curse. Some have made vows to cut ties and never look back. The quote, "blood is thicker than water" isn't based in fiction. Because of the bloodline, our DNA is predisposed to resemble the genetic makeup of our parents more than any others. In essence, it may be more of a battle to not become your parents than the other way around. Most behaviors that come naturally to us have usually been inspired by our parents (formally or informally). To accomplish the task of breaking away, you literally must run from some parts of who you're programmed to be. If you're a Bible-thumper, you'll recognize Deuteronomy 5:9-10

"For I, the Lord your God, am a jealous God, visiting the iniquity of the fathers upon the children to the third and fourth generations of

those who hate Me, but showing mercy to thousands, those who love Me and keep My commandments".

Any good doctor will tell you how vital it is to gather a thorough family history prior to treating a patient. A smart way to predict some elements of my future is to consider what has already occurred in the hierarchy of my bloodline. It's one thing to sever all traditional ties to my father, but when I share his same blood abnormalities - ignoring those details can be to my detriment.

Usually, when we see firefighters running, they are headed in a different direction than we are. We hear it all the time, that first responders run towards danger, while the average person tries desperately to flee it.

 Dr. John D. McConnell

Even the best training doesn't remove fear from dangerous situations. Only a fool has no fear of a fire that's out of control. The more we know about our fears, the better position we're in, even if we are afraid. All first responders know that being afraid isn't a big enough reason not to do their job. Actually, your fear can set the tone for your work ethic. When I first joined the music staff as a worship leader, at a megachurch, It felt a bit overwhelming. I went from singing to a congregation of about two hundred fifty people, to three thousand people. Forgetting song lyrics in a small cafetorium is nothing compared to going silent on a six hundred square-foot stage. My fear of embarrassment every Sunday, might've been equal to my excitement for singing. Fear makes you work hard to be prepared.

No one endeavors to live a meaningless life. In fact, everyone desires to live the best life possible. In common, the time clock is reset daily with twenty-four hours for us all. Despite what happens today, tomorrow affords us a brand-new start. Being an optimistic person, I always try to find a silver lining in every situation. The animals with the shortest lifespan are adult Mayflies, which survive only one day. They have just twenty-four hours to take to the air, find a mate, breed, and die. It could be us, but thankfully, it's not. Not only do we get do-overs every day, but our consciousness isn't stripped away.. We are created with the ability to expand our learning with every moment we're alive. In other words, a seventy-five-year-old person has the wealth of more than twenty-seven thousand days of knowledge. As human beings, our challenge is to convert that knowledge into wisdom. Memory researchers say the capacity of our long-term memory is unlimited, and it can endure

Dr. John D. McConnell

indefinitely. Based on this comparison alone, our purpose is much greater than that of a Mayfly.

In general, there are so many arguments to support how very valuable time is. But the value of time for us as individuals is significantly greater. As we discover our uniqueness, and add wisdom to our understanding, perhaps we can better embrace the passing of time.

Exceed Your Own Expectations

You can never surpass a goal you've not set. We tend to rub elbows with people we feel most comfortable around. The expression, "misery loves company" comes to mind, because it's easier to confide our sad stories to people we consider 'fish from our same pond'. Even when someone tries to hold us accountable, it feels less punitive coming from someone we consider our equal. When we define other people that way, not only do we put them in a box, but we imprison ourselves. Assess where you are by evaluating who you're with. Why are you uncomfortable around people whose visions seem larger than yours? If success is your mission, you should desire relationships with people who've learned to turn their passion into purpose. Their work ethic should encourage you, not alienate you. We must stop waiting to be inspired by people who've made Inspiration famous. The goals you want to achieve aren't achievable if they're only in your head. Write your vision down and keep it in front of you. Give yourself assignments and due dates so that time works in your favor, and not against you. Time is an enemy to those who refuse to keep a calendar. If you can't believe it enough to put it on a calendar, don't expect it to happen.

 Dr. John D. McConnell

Ecclesiastes 9: 11-12

I returned, and saw under the sun that the race is not to the swift, nor the battle to the strong, neither yet bread to the wise, nor yet riches to men of understanding, nor yet favor to men of skill, but TIME, and chance happeneth to them all.

Life for a Mayfly is a sprint, but for us, it's a marathon. Cast your gaze far ahead of you. Partner with time and make incremental steps towards your vision. Procrastinating and waiting are not the same thing. How long are you willing to wait for what you truly believe is yours? Because of the fast-paced world we live in, we feel constant pressure to make things happen. Something my mom said a lot was, "a watched pot never boils". She was trying to help me understand that some things simply require time to develop. Everything can't be hurried. A normal human pregnancy is two hundred eighty days (forty weeks). The cells that form the fetal heart begin to cluster around five to six weeks. The arms and legs also form around the sixth week, and most of the embryo's organs and systems usually take shape by the end of the eighth week. By week ten of pregnancy, the baby's head has become rounder, and can now bend his or her elbows. Toes and fingers lose their webbing, and become longer. The eyelids and external ears continue to develop. At about twelve weeks, the bones of the face are formed. The baby's bones begin to harden, especially in the skull and long bones after thirteen weeks. A baby's head is erect, and his or her eyes can slowly move by week sixteen. By week twenty-two the eyes and lips have developed. A baby's eyes can focus after thirty weeks, and their vision will continue to develop inside and outside the uterus womb.

Dr. John D. McConnell

Instead of trying to short circuit what needs to mature with time, do what's in your power and expect the best outcome. Theodore Roosevelt said, "Do what you can with what you have, where you are." We can only do our part and after the stage is completely set, time makes its reveal. Watching and waiting for water to boil won't make it boil faster. Would you rather things happen right on time, or force an inferior situation to occur? With precision and patience, purpose to continuously gain ground towards your goals. If we approach life this way every day, we'll have no regrets.

Where Are You?

Lots of time, energy, and money gets invested as we're trying to find out who we are, but many of us have trouble grasping where we are. When triggers from your past show up to pull you back into a life you've left, remind yourself where you are. When you're not fully conscious of where you are, your mind can trick you into believing you're where you used to be. Don't go back to responding to situations the same old way. You've worked too hard to be in a different place. Because of the time and energy it took to get to where you are, make it count. Certain people trigger certain behaviors you can't afford to repeat. Whenever you feel that tug to entertain where you've been, remember how hard and long you worked to remove yourself from it. Knowing where you are helps you appreciate where you've been - and hopefully will keep you from ever returning.

Recognize what time it is. Consider all the roles one submits to in life. As children, we submit to our parents. As students, we have teachers. When we enter the workforce, we submit to employers. Every level and stage is a training ground. It's an opportunity for us to imagine what type of leader we'll be when the shoe is on the other foot. Will I be a stern, unemotional basketball coach like the one I had in high school, or will I choose to nurture my athletes? Once I become a husband and father, will I lead my family the same as my dad, or will I do it differently? We're not under certain types of leadership only to complain about it. Time allows us strategies to outlast and survive what we go through. Life will not be denied its cycles. Take note of what's not been effective leadership for you, so when it's your turn to lead, you'll do it better.

Ecclesiastes 3:1-13 NIV

"There is a TIME for everything, and a season for every activity under the heavens: a TIME to be born and a TIME to die, a TIME to plant and a TIME to uproot, a

TIME to kill and a TIME to heal, a TIME to tear down and a TIME to build, a TIME to weep and a TIME to laugh, a TIME to mourn and a TIME to dance, a TIME to scatter stones and a TIME to gather them, a TIME to embrace and a TIME to refrain from embracing, a TIME to search and a TIME to give up, a TIME to keep and a TIME to throw away, a TIME to tear and a TIME to mend, a TIME to be silent and a TIME to speak, a TIME to love and a TIME to hate, a TIME for war and a TIME for peace. What do workers gain from their toil? I have seen the burden God has laid on the human race. He has made everything beautiful in its TIME. He has also set eternity in the human heart; yet no one can fathom what God has done from beginning to end. I know that there is nothing better for people than to be happy and to do good while they live. That each of them may eat and drink, and find

Dr. John D. McConnell

satisfaction in all their toil—this is the gift of God."

As you are identifying and confronting those things that make you afraid, regard some fears as being necessary. What I'll caution you to be fearful of is dying on the vine. Don't allow who you are and what you have to offer to spoil. The only person who can legitimize your reason for being here is you. Fear never finding your purpose. That's a healthy fear because it makes you desperate for change. We must stop huddling with people who do nothing. Imagine a team that goes out on the field but run no plays. Fear being worthless so you'll run far from it. Fear being so tied to poverty that you become jealous when someone you know experiences financial freedom. How entrenched must you be to not celebrate someone else's success? Fear being afraid of giving your kids hope for following their dreams. Don't become the community spokesperson for low expectations. It's a cancer that grows like weeds. Fear becoming a lifelong complainer. The more focus we bring to our problems, the less time we invest in finding solutions. Having problems is not a unique phenomenon, but solving them is a service people pay money for. What we fear is not as much our problem as our response to it.

Dr. John D. McConnell

CHAPTER 10

REDEEMING TIME

Don't make destiny a mystical, far-out thing. We cross paths with it as we journey. It's possible to take too much time waiting for things to be revealed. What is supposed to happen, happens as we're living each day. We redeem time when we're intentional to learn as we go. As each year comes to an end, it seems I hear the same recurring dialogue amongst people. "Wow it seems this year just got started". "Has it been twelve months already"? "This next year will be the best one yet!" I believe God's sense of humor causes Him to end some years early just so He can laugh at how oblivious we seem to it. The popular phrase from an old proverb, "Time waits for no man", is a reality we experience every day. If we had the ability to live six months at a time as different people, we'd gain a broader appreciation for time. I have a brother who is in physical pain most every day. He's lost the vitality in his legs, and

Dr. John D. McConnell

calculates his steps before even getting out of his recliner. I, on the other hand, can walk ten miles every day with no pain whatsoever. But I struggle with clearly seeing where I'm going. What would life be like if I could trade my energy for his eyesight every now and then? If you could periodically wear the highs and lows of other people's lives, you would see how much more you're capable of. You would also use fewer excuses and complain less.

One way to redeem time is to repurpose it to successfully reach menial goals. Most people have lofty dreams, but conquering abject and modest goals infuses momentum for our more prestigious desires. If the only goals we have are gigantic, and require several external factors, it may take years to see them manifest. Meanwhile, you may be unable to point to anything else that hints at productivity. Setting and reaching smaller goals along the way, like losing five pounds, taking a summer class, or painting your bedroom, don't require anyone else's involvement. Once we establish this pattern and consistently get our desired results, we learn how to manage our time more effectively. It must all count for something because we can never get it back. Setting expectations for our time is like creating a budget for our money. We can actually ensure that every minute is accounted for. Put your television and movie watching in your budget. If you realize that's where you're losing a lot of time, reassign it. You'll never be an effective time manager if you can't account for where your time is going. Begin tracking your days out loud – on a whiteboard. Try to recognize any trends or patterns of activity. Of those trends, identify time-killers. Time-killers are activities that are wasteful. They add no value to your life and distract from

Dr. John D. McConnell

your assignments. Decide how you would like to replace those distractions. On your whiteboard, write down how you'd like your time to be distributed each day. This is how you find out if you control your day, or if your day controls you.

Unfortunately, we only start realizing the importance of redeeming time after we've lost so much of it. In our youth, we throw time away like it's meaningless. Most wisdom grows from experiential living, and our youthful years aren't packed with much of it. Even when parents and older mentors try to impart why time management is so important, there is a disconnect. In our twenties and thirties there's a pridefulness that makes us see everyone else's way as wrong. We seek to be trailblazers of unchartered paths, with no regard for time. At that age, our only relationship with time is that of impatience. As a kid, one of the hardest things you'll ever do is wait. There is an amusement park in Kansas City called Worlds of Fun. Each summer we'd go there as a family once a year. I loved the rides like the Zambezi Zinger and the Viking Voyager. We stayed all day. I can even remember the headlights coming on at night on the bumper cars. The only thing I hated about the amusement park was leaving. I dreamed about it all the time. I dreamt about being tall enough the following summer to ride the rides I had been too short to ride before. The waiting made the year so long. I didn't understand why we couldn't afford to go more than once a year. I recall saying things like, "When I'm a grown-up, I'm going to Worlds of Fun as many times as I want. " As children, not only do we suffer from a lack of patience, but we don't know enough about time to respect it as a nonrenewable resource. Unless you've spent an inordinate amount of time around death as a kid, it's hard to comprehend not being here forever.

The true essence of redeeming time is learning to use it in a way that best serves you. Not knowing how to prioritize your life is a conundrum. How does someone with no plans or goals maximize time? Having plenty of time to get to nowhere is an oxymoron. Without a target there's nothing to aim for, so safeguarding time doesn't become important until you have a mission. Where you're headed determines how much time you need. Consider very thoughtfully what you'd like to accomplish in your lifetime. Extra time for some people only exposes their lack of stewardship.

For more than thirty years, I have consulted with many church ministries. As a music ministry coordinator, I've had the assignment to facilitate all things music related for church services. Many churches are small and can't afford to pay singers. Consequently, I have supervised waves of volunteer staff. One of my largest challenges is motivating groups of people to strive for excellence. Paid or unpaid, if you're on the team, the goal should be to win. I think people should be proper stewards of what they commit to. If motivating paid staff to stretch to do more is difficult, imagine the pushback from volunteers. The point I'm attempting to make is, one should purpose to meet the demands of the paths they choose. Go all the way! Be the best steward of what's in your care, and more opportunities will come your way.

Redeeming time also means to do things correctly the first time around. As long as we view the concept of redeeming time as a response, we'll always be behind. Being proactive puts us in a position to solve our problems using the right solutions. Electing

Dr. John D. McConnell

shortcuts for doing things puts us on the path to doing them over and over. Using Inferior parts for our vehicles keeps us broke-down on the side of the road more often. Making only minimum payments on credit accounts extends the length of the loan, while increasing the balance. Some choose a diet of fast foods high in sugar, salt, saturated fat, trans fats, processed ingredients, and calories. In doing so, they take risks that include obesity, insulin resistance, type two diabetes, and various cardiovascular conditions. We choose work time over family time, creating a wedge between us and our children. Some of the very things we choose to save time end up as weapons against us. You may think doing things the best way costs more. Does it really? When you add it all up, are you redeeming anything? I know we can't see into our future. For that reason, we must become very observant of the lives others have lived. Avoid the traps by doing it differently. When thinking about time, consider that quality is sometimes more significant than quantity. What is the benefit of earning more money if I have to use it to pay for therapy for my kids because of my neglect? We must make it all make sense.

When my sons were nine and seven, I purchased a ten-foot basketball hoop from Walmart for around three hundred dollars. I remember it took me an entire weekend to assemble. After eighteen or so months, the Texas sun, heat, and wind caused it to lean awkwardly. I sacrificed another three hundred dollars and a full weekend to do it all again when my oldest turned eleven. I realized a pattern of the hoops needing to be replaced every two years. After the fifth replacement, and more than fifteen hundred dollars, I hired a company to install an alloy steel regulation-size basketball hoop with a lifetime warranty for the price of the five temporary hoops.

For ten years I was stuck in a pattern of trying to spend the least amount, while hoping for maximum satisfaction. I wish someone had stepped up and challenged me on my thinking back then. Perhaps it would have assisted me in redeeming lots of energy, money, and time.

I have lived long enough to see time turn into something much more than it used to be. Many define time as an irreversible succession of events from the past present, and future, regarded as a whole. I see time as a continuum, that changes as I change. It's fixed as in hours, days, months, and years – but for some of us, it bends. We bend time by exploiting its parameters. I'm not talking science fiction, like "The Matrix". Instead of being confined by it, we can use it to transform. When I was a little boy, my church choir sang a song titled, "Redeemed". The lyrics talked about being washed in the blood of the lamb.

In the Bible, Isaiah chapter 1, verse 18 says "Come now, and let us reason together saith the Lord. Though your sins be as scarlet, they shall be as white as snow. Though they be red like Crimson they shall be as wool".

The scripture means that by choosing Jesus as savior, He will cause the transgressions of your life to be of non-effect. He offers us a clean slate - exchanging our darkness for His light. Redeem time by simply deciding that you're only going to do things you desire to do. I know this sounds bold, but much of our empowerment comes from taking a stand. When we're inundated with the schedules, others put us on, we have no time to create our own. I can already hear the retort. "Everyone can't afford to only do what they want to do". The seed for who you want to be and where you want to go starts with your declaration. Say it with your mouth until you can see it with your imagination, then bring it to life. Not only the financially rich travel the world. There are too many examples in this world of people winning against the odds. That will forever be the case, because 'where there's a will, there's a way'. Aren't you tired of spending every day advancing the agenda of others? You must find a balance that allows you to give to others without totally giving yourself away. An unfulfilled you can easily become a bitter you.

Relinquish Old Pursuits

Recently, I ran into a problem with my laptop running out of memory. In addition to all of the programs I have installed, I had several folders on my desktop filled with files I've not used in years. The clutter began to affect my processing speed and every now and then, my system imposed a forced shutdown to improve its performance. It was necessary for me to do a purge to restore the capabilities of my laptop. It was a tedious process, but as I opened each folder, I saw hundreds of documents and photos from my distant past. It was like they were incarcerated on my desktop, waiting in line to be paroled back into the mainstream of my life. At least eighty-five percent of what was there had no relationship to the life I'm currently living. I immediately sentenced those files for deletion. Allowing them to remain would continue draining processing power, vital to my operating system.

Many people are hanging onto things that no longer represent the pattern of their life. We keep our skinny clothes in the closet from years ago, that (unless we time travel) we'll most likely never be able to wear again. There is a fear about letting certain things go. It's like admitting you've lost. Letting go of old things doesn't always mean you've lost a battle. Sometimes releasing things is simply what it looks like when attempting to capture something new. Preparation must be part of the process for adding to our lives. Only the unwise would refurnish a house without first removing the old furniture. Everything from our past won't fit in our future. Redeem time by narrowing your focus. If the playbook you're trying to use was manufactured for goals you no longer have, your system is overdue for an update. Sync your strategies with the path you're on today, and let go of what has not worked. This will help to streamline your process, and hopefully improve your timeline.

I'm always going to advocate for integrity. However, if you're trying to fulfill promises you made years ago, they may not still be binding. The vows we take in marriage are until death. But it's impossible to hold, honor, and cherish someone who has decided to no longer be held, honored, or cherished by you. If I respond, yes, to my father's dying request that I move to Florida and take over his apple orchard, am I bound by that no matter what? Inevitably, we all face situations we must yield to. It's admirable when we enter commitments we know at face value will be difficult. I believe most people have every intention of honoring the pledges they make. The end of the line isn't always identifiable. The size of our investment helps us vote "stay-in", or "get-out". When honoring vows is at the top of your character profile, to not follow through, feels like missing the mark. Rather than yielding to the overwhelming evidence supporting cutting ties, we hold on. Holding onto things beyond our ability to affect positively, robs us of whatever we throw at it. Sometimes money, mental

Dr. John D. McConnell

energy, emotions, and time are all leveraged for a bucket with holes in it. It's sometimes hard to recognize when you're the one being spread then. It's not always what we've verbally committed to that keeps us in limbo. Just being aware of expectations our families have had for us since childhood can be a distraction. If we allow everyone to have a slice of us, there will be nothing left. We must embrace that we can't be all things for all people. We're only allocated a certain amount of time. Stop wasting years trying to fit your roundness into a square peg. No matter what story you tell yourself, you were not designed to fit that mold. Don't be saddened by that. It simply means you've not yet discovered your destiny. You'll never have to contort or conform to the greatness you're destined for. When you cross paths with it, no modifications will be required - as you were made for it, and it for you.

The most emphatic way I know of to redeem time is to control it. Begin creating your own timeline for accomplishments. Some systems aren't designed to change, and no matter how patient we are in following protocol, those with the most power may never choose us. Skip to the front of the line by taking the power out of their hands. Start your own band and begin to move to the beat of your new drummer. Taking the power sometimes means you must unplug from where you are and tap into a source that has the nutrients you require. As a teenager, I remember my dad schooling me on loyalty and commitment. He was explaining that once you establish a relationship with an organization, over time, they get to know you as an individual. He said, "In most cases, if you stick with them, they'll stick with you". My dad worked for the same company for thirty-two years and I understood all that

Dr. John D. McConnell

he was implying. I've lived that way, even in regard to creditors I maintain accounts with. I know what it is to be loyal, but I've also watched the world turn. There was a time when if your account was well maintained, your heat would not be shut off in the coldest part of winter due to a missed payment. Today, unless there are laws in your state to prevent such a thing, your family will freeze to death if your account is delinquent. Loyalty and commitment still work the same - just not in all circles. What does betting on you look like? Maybe you've never been the one responsible for creating budgets and finding ways to meet them. It's scary because it's risky. Before, you never felt the weight of the risk. Now you're experiencing a different kind of weight. It's the weight of the wait. Years are passing you by with no consideration for promotion. Waiting becomes unsustainable when there's no more time to lose! Turn the tables by setting the narrative. Put dates on the wall and erase the word "tentative". Let's elevate our thinking from "TBD" to "right now". The world is much too large to only give one company the opportunity to sleep on your greatness. There are billions who've not met you. Hundreds more may decide you're not what they're looking for. So what? You only need one door to open. Things won't automatically happen just because you've become more aggressive with your timeline. You dramatically decrease your odds when your stance becomes less passive. Expectations go sky high when dates are on the calendar. The more specific we are about when we say things will happen forces us to act like it is so. What bride sends out wedding invitations without corresponding actions? You'd be baffled if she didn't know her wedding colors only weeks before her big day. I'm not suggesting you play a

Dr. John D. McConnell

game with your mind, trying to trick it to believe something that will never occur. I'm challenging you to step into a role your life now depends on. The mistake we make as kids is to believe that time is a luxury. The longer we live, the more the cover gets pulled back to reveal how much time we've wasted. That luxury becomes taxed heavily in our golden years.

As of 2024, the average lifespan of a male in the United States is seventy-four years. People on average spend ninety thousand hours at work over their lifetime. That's equivalent to 10.2 years. Fourteen percent of a man's life is spent on the job. The federal reserve's most recent data reveals that the average American has only $65,000 in retirement savings. Most adults are unaware of how to make money work for them. If we truly want to redeem time as it relates to financial freedom, we must advocate on behalf of children. Their high school education must include money market literacy. Before they enter the workforce, our kids must be taught to comprehend certain financial principles and concepts, such as the time value of money, managing debt and financial planning, and compound interest. Financial literacy is a tool for avoiding poor financial decisions and retiring broke. After spending fourteen percent of your lifetime on an assembly line, in a warehouse, on a tuna boat, in a coal mine, in a factory, or in the military - your reward should be to retire as a millionaire.

Dr. John D. McConnell

ABOUT THE AUTHOR

DR. JOHN DAVID MCCONNELL

Dr. John David McConnell is the owner of
Prolyric Productions Publishing Company.
Born and raised in Kansas City Kansas, John

received his Bachelor of Science degree at Saint Mary College in Leavenworth, Kansas. John taught grades 2 through 8 over the span of his 27-year career as a public-school educator. 20 of those years were with the Houston Independent School District.

In 2016 John received his doctorate in sacred music from Christian Bible Institute & Seminary. His war chest of badges includes Christian, father of two sons, educator, actor, singer, songwriter, worship-leader, Certified Christian Counselor, and author. John exited his teaching career in 2022, and is currently pursuing his literary and songwriting careers full-time.

To Contact John McConnell:
Johndmac4@aol.com
832-865-0260

Printed in the United States
by Baker & Taylor Publisher Services